THE FOUR ESSENTIALS OF
CONFLICT RESOLUTION

How to Resolve Just About Any Conflict Over Just About Anything With Just About Anybody

THE FOUR ESSENTIALS OF CONFLICT RESOLUTION

How to Resolve Just About Any Conflict Over Just About Anything With Just About Anybody

Adam Lodzinski, Ph.D.

The Conflict Resolving Network Inc.

Published by The Conflict Resolving Network Inc.
120 Adelaide Street West, Suite 2500,
Toronto, Ontario, Canada, M5H 1T1
www.theconflictresolvingnetwork.com

Editors: Barbara Palmer editor@theconflictresolvingnetwork.com
Evert Akkerman info@xnlhr.com
Priscilla Babin pris.babin@rogers.com

Cover and book design: David Moratto www.davidmoratto.com

First edition.
Printed in Canada.

ISBN: 978-0-9866035-1-8 (Paperback)

Disclaimer

The Four Essentials of Conflict Resolution: How to Resolve Just About Any Conflict Over Just About Anything With Just About Anybody, its information, ideas and suggestions, are provided for informational purposes only. It is not intended to be professional advice, nor does it serve as a substitute for professional advice (whether psychological, legal or otherwise). The information and strategies contained herein may not be suitable for every situation and results may differ for each individual. If you require advice on a specific matter, the services of an appropriate professional should be sought.

The publisher and the author of this book make no representations or warranties of any kind, express or implied, for any particular purpose, and expressly disclaim all representations and warranties, including without limitation any representations or warranties related to the quality, accuracy, reliability, suitability, completeness or appropriateness of the information or strategies contained herein, the accuracy of any opinions or information presented, any particular results that may be achieved by following/implementing the strategies contained herein or fitness for any particular purpose, and no such representations or warranties shall be created or extended by sales or promotional materials.

Further, third-party websites listed or referenced herein may have changed or disappeared between the time that this book was written and when it is read. In no event shall the publisher or author be responsible for the information contained on such sites, or your use of or inability to use such sites.

The publisher and the author of this book assume no responsibility whatsoever for any loss or damage of any kind suffered or incurred by any person making use of or relying on the information or strategies contained herein or on any third-party websites referenced herein. Any use of such information or strategies contained herein is at your own risk.

*To my family, without whose love and support this
book could never have been written.*

CONTENTS

PREFACE *1*

What's Coming Up in the Chapters Ahead *2*

CHAPTER 1 The Four Essentials of Conflict and Conflict Resolution *5*

1.1 The Four Essentials of Conflict *5*
1.2 The Four Essentials of Conflict Resolution *20*

CHAPTER 2 The Stages of Conflict and Steps of Conflict Resolution . . . *23*

2.1 The Four Stages of Conflict *24*
2.2 The Four Steps of Conflict Resolution *39*
2.3 Some Helpful Things to Bear in Mind Going Forward *44*

CHAPTER 3 When in Conflict Emotion Powers, Thinking Guides *51*

3.1 Emotion Powers, Thinking Guides *52*
3.2 The Power of Emotion *53*
3.3 The Helpful Qualities of Thinking *58*
3.4 The Qualities of Thinking that Can Make it Unhelpful *60*
3.5 Emotional Triggers *62*
3.6 Relationship Flashpoints and Fireworks *65*
3.7 Putting Relationship Fireworks and Flashpoints into Words *67*
3.7.1 Putting Relationship Fireworks into Words *70*
3.7.2 Putting Relationship Flashpoints into Words *76*

CHAPTER 4 Conflict-Prone Relationships *87*

4.1 Strained Relationships *88*
4.2 Draining Relationships *89*
4.3 Ambivalent Relationships *90*
4.4 Stretched Relationships *99*
4.5 Square-Peg-Round-Hole Relationships *101*
4.6 Lop-sided Relationships *104*
4.7 Troubling Triads: Lop-sided Three-Way Relationships *107*
4.8 Uncharted Territory Relationships *110*
4.9 Some Concluding Thoughts on Conflict-Prone Relationships . . *110*

CHAPTER 5 Do You Want To Resolve This Conflict? *115*

5.1 Overview of the Questions to Ask Yourself *118*
5.1.1 Tangible Costs and Benefits *119*
5.1.2 Psychological Costs and Benefits *121*
5.1.3 The Future *126*
5.2 How to Get the Most Out of the Decision-Guiding Questions . . . *128*
5.3 The Benefits, Costs and Future of Resolving Your Conflict:
The "Yes, Resolve" Triangle *131*
5.3.1 Questions About the Immediate Benefits of
Resolving Your Conflict *131*
5.3.2 Questions About the Possible Future Benefits of
Resolving Your Conflict *135*
5.3.3 Questions About the Immediate Costs of
Resolving Your Conflict *141*
5.3.4 Questions About the Possible Future Costs of
Resolving Your Conflict *146*
5.4 The Costs, Benefits and Future of Not Resolving Your Conflict:
The "No, Don't Resolve" Triangle *150*
5.4.1 Questions About the Immediate Costs of
NOT Resolving Your Conflict *150*
5.4.2 Questions About the Possible Future Costs of
NOT Resolving Your Conflict *155*

5.4.3 Questions About the Immediate Benefits of
NOT Resolving Your Conflict *158*

5.4.4 Questions About the Possible Future Benefits of
NOT Resolving Your Conflict *161*

5.5 Coming to Your Decision. *164*

CHAPTER 6 How to Navigate the Resolution of Your Conflict *167*

6.1 One More Important Use for the
Cost-Benefit-Future Triangle *168*

6.2 Communicating When in Conflict *171*

6.3 Working Through the Four Steps of the Conflict Resolution
Process–Step One: Offering an Olive Branch *179*

6.3.1 Apologizing *183*

6.4 Step Two: Conflict Unpacking *194*

6.4.1 Unpacking with the Four Essentials *195*

6.5 Step Three: Disagreement Resolution. *203*

6.5.1 Values and Values Conflicts *207*

6.5.2 Relationship Rearranging. *224*

6.6 Step Four: Reconciliation and Celebration *228*

6.6.1 On Forgiving and Asking for Forgiveness *230*

6.7 Family, Friends, and Others in Conflict Resolution *233*

CONCLUDING THOUGHTS *235*

Acknowledgments *239*

Your Feedback is Welcomed!. *241*

About the Author *243*

PREFACE

This is a book for everyone. I've written it to help you get the most out of your relationships with those who matter most in your life. If there's one thing that can ruin any relationship, it's too many conflicts; and if there's one thing that can improve any relationship, it's learning how to resolve them.

Although conflict is an inevitable part of life and perfectly natural in the ebb and flow of any relationship, it becomes a problem if the things people do when in conflict generate more animosity, distress, suffering and turmoil than whatever sparked the conflict in the first place. Bad decisions and big mistakes can accompany conflict; and sometimes, very serious, costly, and irreparable ones. We've all seen lives and careers ruined because tempers were lost, and arguments went too far. We've seen unresolved conflict tear apart couples, families, friends, and even businesses—and often needlessly so, because a lot of the time these conflicts could have been de-escalated sooner, resolved, or even prevented.

Of course, conflict isn't always a bad thing! The good news is, when successfully resolved, conflict can and often does strengthen relationships and helps build new common ground from which to move forward. With every successful resolution, your relationships can become deeper and more fulfilling. Indeed, the quality of any relationship you have with anyone depends not on the absence of conflict, but on how well the two of you resolve it when it does arise. After all, while it is true that conflict sometimes brings out the worst in us, its successful resolution has the potential to bring out the best.

Simply put, my aim in this book is to share with you what I've learned throughout my career helping people resolve conflicts. This book covers what you need to know and do to resolve whatever conflicts you have now, as well as conflicts you're likely to have. It also contains many new ideas that I'm sure you'll be able to relate to and use to resolve almost any conflict, with almost anybody, over almost anything. It's also the kind of book you can read on your own, or with someone you care about, and return to whenever you need to.

One last thing: There are almost two hundred countries in the world and over seven thousand languages spoken, representing millions of ways of viewing conflict and how to resolve it. So, wherever you are from and whatever your culture and language and background is, I sincerely invite you to take from my book what works for you. It is my deepest hope that what you'll learn in this book will at least in some small way not only help reduce the number of conflicts that arise in your life—and help you resolve them when they do—but that it will also help you help those who matter the most in your life to resolve and prevent theirs.

Adam Lodzinski, Ph.D.
Toronto, Ontario
March 2023

What's Coming Up in the Chapters Ahead...

Before we begin, let me give you a brief overview of each of the six chapters of this book. In Chapter 1, I'll cover the key ideas that form the book's foundation—the four essentials of conflict and its resolution: Loss, intent, violation, and responsibility. Chapter 2 provides a bird's eye view of the four stages of conflict as well as the four steps of conflict resolution. Understanding these stages and steps, along with what's presented in this chapter, prepares you for what's to come in Chapters 3, 4, 5, and 6. Chapter 3 helps you understand the potent mix of thoughts and feelings that can arise in conflict. Chapter 4 covers eight conflict-prone relationships that are important to be mindful of. Chapter 5 helps you answer for yourself that all-important—and often very tough—question (and one that I've never seen addressed in any book on conflict resolution), namely, whether or not you want to resolve your conflict in the first place. Lastly, Chapter 6 brings it all together, focusing on what you need to know and do to successfully navigate each step of the conflict resolution process.

THE FOUR ESSENTIALS OF CONFLICT AND CONFLICT RESOLUTION

1.1 THE FOUR ESSENTIALS OF CONFLICT

Conflict has been variously defined by different experts, but all definitions land on the notion that conflict arises from incompatible actions or goals between two people that result in one person's gain being the other person's loss. This definition is a helpful starting point, but it is not detailed enough for our purposes. In this book, I define conflict as any situation in which what one person does:

1. causes a **loss** of something for the other person, whether that loss is tangible or psychological or both, and
2. looks like it was done **intentionally**, and
3. **violates** the "rules" of the relationship, and
4. is something that either one or both people can be held **responsible** for.

I call these the four essentials of conflict because all four of them —loss, intent, violation, and responsibility—must be present for there to be a conflict. If any one of these essentials is missing, there's either less potential for conflict or no conflict at all.

- If what someone does (or doesn't do) costs you nothing and you haven't lost anything (either psychologically or tangibly) then there's no reason for conflict.

- If what someone does causes you to lose something, but whatever they did, they did unintentionally (i.e., it's clearly accidental, not deliberate or the result of a misunderstanding of some kind), then the potential for conflict dissipates quickly.
- Even if you've lost something, if it was lost fair and square according to the rules you both abide by in whatever kind of relationship you're in (e.g., there's been no cheating or unfair advantage), then there's no conflict either—you may be in a rivalry, a contest, or a competition, but not a conflict.
- Finally, if you can't blame the other person outright for your loss, or if neither of you can be blamed for what happened, then the potential for conflict is considerably lessened.

Keep in mind that all four essentials depend to varying degrees on interpretation and perception; that is, how you see each one. To be specific: How you see what's been lost and how big a loss it is; what you think the other person intended in doing what they did to cause your loss; what violation occurred and how serious this violation is and, finally, who you see as responsible or at fault (and to what extent). More on this later in this chapter; in the meantime, let's take some time to examine what constitutes loss, intent, violation, and responsibility in more detail. As you read this section, I invite you to reflect on one or more past conflicts or one that you are in now.

Want an easy way of remembering the four essentials? Think LIVR.
Loss + Intent + Violation + Responsibility (LIVR) = Conflict

---

1. *Loss*

The first essential or necessary condition for conflict is loss. You experience a loss under one or more of three conditions: First, if someone takes something you value away from you without giving you enough—or anything—in return; second, if someone does something to you that you don't want to have done to you; or third, if someone withholds, refuses, or neglects to give you something that you do want, expect, or believe you are owed or deserve. *Note that in all three scenarios, the loss comes at some <u>cost</u> to you, for example:*

- When someone takes something of value away from you, it can cost you something to get it back or replace it.
- When someone does something to you that you don't want to have done to you, there's not only an emotional cost to you (e.g., you feel betrayed), but it can also cost you time, money, or effort to recover from what was done.
- When someone withholds, refuses, or neglects to give you something that you do want, expect, or believe you are owed or deserve, it costs you something to live without it or make up for its absence.

You know there's a loss when there's a cost.

Your losses and costs can be tangible, psychological, or both. Tangible losses include the loss of money, personal property, and time (e.g., the time and money it will take to repair what's been damaged or recover what was taken from you). Physical injury or a downturn in your health and well-being are also tangible losses. The loss of a chance at something (e.g., not being told about a job opening) or not receiving money or property you're entitled to are also tangible.

Psychological loss refers to the emotional cost to you of what someone did. This includes the cost of having to endure such feelings as shock, dismay, anger, resentment, frustration, sadness, disappointment, embarrassment, or grief. Psychological loss refers not only to the emotional toll of enduring such feelings but also to the effort in mental energy of trying to cope with, resist or push these away—all of which can be exhausting after a while.

Note too that sometimes psychological loss can become tangible, as when, because of the stress of a conflict, for example, you start to suffer physical symptoms such as trouble sleeping, losing your appetite, getting headaches, and the like.

Psychological loss almost always accompanies a tangible loss (i.e., the pain and suffering from a tangible loss)—or vice versa—as noted above. But psychological loss can also be experienced without tangible loss, for instance, when someone puts you down, snubs you, or tries—but fails—to do something that could have resulted in a tangible loss. Psychological loss also stems from having to deal with a change in the way people see you because of what someone has said about you (e.g., by spreading rumors or lies).

Finally, psychological loss without tangible loss can also be felt when you want, expect, hope, or wish someone treated you a certain way, but they don't. This often feels like a loss even though, strictly speaking, it is not a loss if nothing was ever promised to you or, for that matter, taken away from you. *Not getting what you want—or are longing for—from someone is not the same thing as losing what you already have. But dashed hopes (e.g., unrequited love) and unfulfilled hopes or expectations, even if they are unfounded, often feel like a loss—sometimes a very big one—and lie at the heart of many a conflict.*

Before moving on, what can ease psychological loss, regardless of whether it is tied to a tangible one or not? Several things can:

- First and foremost, both love and liking for the other person have the potential of lessening psychological loss, at least up to a point.
- Psychological loss can be lessened if there are enough good things about the relationship that make up for whatever the loss happens to be.
- Psychological loss can also be reduced when you feel—rightly or wrongly—that it is your role in the relationship or that you have an obligation to endure the emotional cost to you of whatever the other person does.
- Psychological loss can also be eased if, for whatever reason—again, rightly or wrongly—you believe you deserved it, or "had it coming," or that you owe the other person something.
- As they say, time heals all wounds. All emotions fade over time, and, like any emotion, the sense of loss also diminishes. Although time can and often does reduce psychological loss, in some cases—depending on the loss—time may never completely erase it.
- Another factor that can mitigate psychological loss is that you've gotten used to it; that is to say, you've gotten used to living without whatever it was you once had.

Getting used to a loss and being immune to the effects of that loss are two different things. Just because you may have gotten used to having lost something, or more simply, have gotten used to living without it, this does not necessarily mean that you're immune to the effects of living with that loss. As an example, if the loss is significant enough, you can still feel sad, hurt, or resentful every time you're reminded of what it was that you once had.

What can worsen or intensify psychological loss? Usually, it's the size of the tangible loss; that is, the greater the tangible loss, the greater the psychological loss is likely to be. However, in addition to whatever the magnitude of a tangible loss is, there are several ways by which psychological loss can be made worse.

- Psychological loss can be worsened if, plainly and simply, you're having a bad day, you're stressed out or feeling on edge, feeling drained or depleted.
- Psychological loss can also be worsened the more the other person benefits from whatever it was that they gained at your expense. This is especially so if they've gotten away scot-free!
- Psychological loss can be magnified when, even if you've both suffered losses, you don't feel you've yet evened the score or that you may never be able to.
- Another way psychological loss can be made worse is if what the other person did comes like a thunderbolt "out of the blue" and therefore is a complete shock and surprise to you and feels like a complete betrayal. It's even worse if you've been a good friend and done the other person many favors, and they are indebted to you (i.e., they owe you something to begin with).
- Psychological loss also tends to be magnified if the other person denies, minimizes, or dismisses your loss (e.g., "What are you so upset about? It's no big deal.") or suggests there is something wrong with you for feeling a loss in the first place (e.g., "You're being too sensitive.").
- Psychological loss can be greater when there is an audience, or witnesses, to what happened (e.g., being embarrassed in front of others or knowing that everyone will hear about what happened). Children and teenagers are especially sensitive to this. An audience can not only be in-person but can also be online, and loss can be

intensified if the person knows that someone is recording what is going on and that their recording could be posted on social media.

- Loss can also be made worse when it directly or indirectly also impacts the people you love, or for that matter, anyone you care about.

Even if you don't personally and directly experience a loss, if a loss occurs to someone you love or care about, there's potential for conflict with whoever you're sure is responsible.

- This may sound a bit odd to you, but psychological loss can be worsened when you care about the other person so much that you suffer by seeing them suffer—even if it's all because of a conflict they started.

- Finally, loss is magnified when you've got such an accumulated sense of loss (e.g., you feel a lot of anger, resentment, disappointment, etc.) from previous conflicts with the other person that you are plainly and simply fed up. You might be fed up with all the conflict you've been having, as well as sick and tired of the relationship and all that it's costing you emotionally. What can happen then is that when that person causes yet another loss for you, it feels like a much greater loss than it would have otherwise. In other words, as the saying goes, it's the "straw that breaks the camel's back." So, what happens? There's a good chance that you "snap" … you "lose it" … you "go ballistic"—an experience that I'm sure each and every one of you reading this book can relate to.

Why Loss is So Central to Conflict

There are two related reasons why loss is so important to conflict. The first is because loss brings unfairness and inequity to any relationship, which most people find nearly impossible to tolerate and feel compelled—sooner or later—to set right. This, of course, then paves the way for escalation; so, in a nutshell, loss, inequity, and unfairness form the birthplace of conflict. Note that ordinary language reflects our sensitivity to loss, debt, inequity, and unfairness, as when we hear people say:

> "I am in your debt."
> "What can I do to make it up to you?"
> "Don't get mad, get even."
> "You're going to get yours!"
> "This will cost you!"
> "You'd better take back what you just said to me!"
> "What have I done to deserve this?"
> "You owe me an apology."

The greater the loss, the greater the inequity, and the greater the inequity, the greater the potential for conflict!

The second thing that ties loss so closely to conflict is that loss throws the plusses and minuses of your relationship out of kilter. There are many aspects to any kind of relationship and many ingredients that go into the making of a successful one. At the most fundamental level, however, and from the point of view of understanding the impact of loss, there are three ingredients that need to be present for many kinds of relationships to work—including romantic relationships, friendships, business relationships, etc. First, there must be plusses to the relationship for both of you; second, the plusses must outweigh the minuses for both of you; and third, you both must feel an overall sense of fairness about your relationship;

that is, both of you must feel that each is contributing their fair share and getting their fair share in return.

Of course, far more goes into the making of most relationships—especially close ones—than plusses, minuses, and fairness (love or liking as well as trust, respect, commitment, communication, and honesty are just some ingredients that spring immediately to mind). I know that talking about relationships in terms like plusses and minuses (or pros and cons, costs and benefits, and the like) can sound a bit cold and oversimplified. Indeed, most of the time, most people don't think of their relationships in these terms; however, when in conflict, relationship plusses, minuses, and fairness are exactly what come into question and what both people home in on.

To illustrate, with respect to the importance of plusses, just think for a moment how long you'd stay at a job if your boss stopped paying you; or how long you'd keep doing someone favors if none were ever returned; or just how long you'd want to stay in a romantic relationship with a partner who neglected you, ignored your desires and trampled on your hopes and dreams? *In other words, both of you must get something out of any kind of relationship to want to stay in it.*

With respect to minuses, being in any relationship has its costs (time, money, and effort, to name a few). Why? Because no one is perfect: There are no perfect families, no perfect romantic partners, no perfect friends, and no perfect places to work or people to work with, so no match is perfect. What this means is that give and take will always be required by both people in any kind of relationship. If you feel that what you must put into (or put up with in) a relationship (which adds to its minuses) is not worth what you're getting out of it (its plusses), then it's only natural that you won't want to stay in it for long.

I'll delve into relationship minuses and plusses and their connection to both tangible and psychological costs and benefits in much more detail in Chapter 5.

Finally, when it comes to relationship fairness, if you feel that you're not getting your fair share out of the relationship and at the same time feel that you're putting more than your fair share into it, you'll feel short-changed. For example, if you're the one who's been doing most of the giving, continually self-sacrificing to give the other person what they need or want at your expense (i.e., over-accommodating), and making a much bigger effort to keep the relationship afloat, then sooner or later it's only natural that you will feel angry and resentful.

So, to sum up, because of loss, it's likely that you'll get less out of a relationship than you did before. Also, depending on how the conflict unfolds and whether it is resolved, the relationship may now cost you more than it did before (i.e., there will be more minuses that you have to endure). Furthermore, if it looks like you're going to have to make more of an effort to keep the relationship going, this adds to the unfairness of the relationship, and understandably, your resentment will likely grow, as will the potential—sooner or later—for conflict.

If a loss is the root of conflict, then the three other essentials—intent, violation, and responsibility—are its soil.

---

2. Intent

The second essential or necessary condition for conflict to arise is that you believe that what the other person did was both deliberate and aimed at you personally. The potential for conflict is considerably reduced if you believe that what the other person did was accidental or unintentional and that no harm was meant.

Determining intent can be tricky because it is sometimes hard to know for sure what someone's intention was despite what they tell us. For example, if you can't say "I didn't do it" (because it's obvious you did), at least you can say "I didn't mean it." We all know this sort of thing is easy and tempting to say if you want to wiggle out of a conflict or some other awkward situation. Sometimes we can give the other person the benefit of the doubt, and sometimes we can't; when we can, the potential for conflict is lessened.

Neglectfulness, thoughtlessness, and even forgetfulness are a case in point. For instance, let's say your best friend doesn't offer to help you with something important. You'd be disappointed, you may well feel hurt, and you might also feel angry and resentful, especially if you'd have happily offered to help them if it were you.

Presumably, this lapse wasn't deliberate. Or was it? Did they completely forget about it? Or did it cross their mind, and did they decide to not offer their help (hoping you would not ask)? You just don't know. Sometimes you can give the other person the full benefit of the doubt, and sometimes you can't. If you can, the potential for conflict is nearly zero or zero. If you can't give them the full benefit of the doubt, the potential for conflict is reduced to the extent that you can.

The potential for conflict can also be somewhat lessened if what was done was done purely on impulse and not premeditated (providing it was not too serious a violation in the first place and an apology for it came quickly). Conflict can also be mitigated if what the other person did was well-intentioned but came out wrong (e.g., well-intentioned criticism that sounded harsh; well-intentioned advice that sounded a bit condescending, nosey, bossy, or preachy). Conflict can be diminished as well when there was a well-founded, balanced, and well-intentioned reason motivated by a sincere rationale for doing whatever caused the loss (e.g., "I didn't tell you because I didn't want to hurt your feelings." "I didn't want to worry you.").

Finally, when there's no ill will at all, and it's not personal, even if there's psychological or tangible loss (e.g., a layoff at a business because of an economic downturn), then the potential for conflict is considerably lessened. So as long as it's not personal, even if there are hard feelings, there's a lesser chance of a conflict erupting.

The impact of intent is made worse when something was clearly done with provocation or malice in mind (and likely with forethought as well) to inflict tangible or psychological loss. Indeed, the greater the ill will behind the intent, the greater the potential for conflict. As it does with loss and inequity, everyday language reflects our sensitivity to someone's intent:

> "I didn't mean it."
> "I didn't want this to happen."
> "I meant no harm."
> "I meant well; it just came out wrong."
> "It's nothing personal—this is purely a business decision."
> "I was just kidding."
> "I was only trying to be funny."
> "I was only trying to help."
> "It was an honest mistake."

3. *Violation*

The third essential condition for conflict to arise is when the other person does something that violates what you've assumed to be one of the rules you agreed to about what's OK to do and what's not OK to do in your relationship. All relationships have stated as well as unstated boundaries, rules, and expectations. These boundaries, rules, and expectations are typically based on shared social customs, norms, values, or codes of conduct, whether formal (e.g., a professional code of conduct) or informal (e.g., "bro code").

Conflict can stem from mistaken assumptions or misunderstandings over how you're supposed to treat one another and what has—or has not—been agreed to in this regard. This situation can arise when you don't know each other well, or at least well enough, to know exactly what each other's customs, values, or relationship rules and expectations are.

As everyone knows, early on in any relationship, whether it be a business relationship, a friendship, or a romantic relationship, a good deal of time is spent looking for things that you have in common as a way of checking for compatibility. There are many aspects of compatibility, and most of them depend on the nature of the relationship; however, one very important aspect of compatibility in most relationships is shared values.

Although you might not ask directly about values, you might do so indirectly by asking about each other's backgrounds, life experiences, passions, interests, opinions, as well as likes (e.g., do you like the same movies?), and dislikes (e.g., do you complain about the same things? Or the same people?). Questions like these shed light on what one another's values are and possibly more; for example, what each other's contributions and expectations might be in any future relationship you might have.

Violation can also occur when two people don't see the nature of their relationship in the same way (e.g., one person sees the relationship as a budding romance, while the other views it as a budding friendship). This situation is made worse if they don't know that they don't agree because they've never openly talked about it (or if they did, the message—one way or the other—did not get through). What can happen then is that because the relationship is viewed differently by both people, what is seen as being OK to do (and even expected) from the point of view of one person is not OK from the point of view of the other.

Violation can be mitigated (in some cases completely) when one person did not and could not have known that their action violates one of the other person's rules or expectations in the first place. This commonly arises when children misbehave and simply don't know that what they did is misbehavior or when someone commits a social gaffe, not realizing that what they did was, under the circumstances, a faux pas.

**We all have lines we will not cross. We also all have lines
we do not want anyone to cross against us.**

What makes violation worse? Sometimes rules can be bent, boundaries can be crossed, and expectations changed, but only with the other person's permission (e.g., "May I ask you a personal question? "Can I ask you for a favor?" or "Can I tell you what I really think?" So, the first thing that makes violation worse is when permission was not asked for, or, if asked for, not granted.

Violation is also made worse when it is obvious that the other person knew their action was a violation of the rules and expectations of your relationship (made even worse if it's not the first time it's happened). Another way that violation is made worse is when the rule or expectation that was violated is grounded in a value you hold deeply; for example, faithfulness, honesty (that you will never lie to one another), or support (you will always have "each other's back"). Violating a deeply held and cherished value can be a grievous breach of trust that can inflict an especially painful emotional wound.

Finally, violation is made worse when it is discovered rather than admitted to. For instance, all things being equal, it is easier to forgive someone who admits to having lied to you than it is to forgive someone whose lie you uncover on your own or find out about from someone else.

As with inequity and intent, ordinary language reflects our sensitivity to violation; for example, when we hear people say:

> "How dare you speak to me in that way?"
> "That was totally out of line."
> "That's no way to treat your...!"
> "That's not what we agreed to."
> "This is not what I signed up for."

"That topic is off limits!"
"What gives you the right to...?"

The words violation and violence share the same root.

---

4. Responsibility

The fourth essential condition for conflict to arise is that whoever caused your loss can be held personally responsible for it. While it is often obvious who caused your loss, the question of the degree to which they are responsible for what they did (i.e., are at fault and can be blamed) is sometimes difficult to answer definitively. One reason for this is that we assign blame or responsibility based on how much control or choice we believe the other person had over what they could and couldn't do. That is why, for example, the person who was simply following their boss' orders cannot be held as responsible for their actions as the boss who gave the orders, or why it's easier to excuse a 4-year-old's temper tantrum than it is a 40-year-old's.

The question of responsibility is often complicated and nuanced. How much a person can or should be held responsible for their actions tends to be a matter of degree, with extenuating circumstances that should be considered. In any case, as I said earlier, if you can't blame the other person outright for all your loss, or if the two of you can share the blame for it, the potential for conflict is considerably lessened.

Just as with loss, intent, and violation, ordinary language reflects the importance of the question of personal responsibility, as when we hear people say:

"I didn't do it!"
"You made me do it."
"You started it!"
"I don't make the rules."

"I totally 'lost it'—I didn't know what I was doing!"

"I was left with no option—what else could I do?"

"I'm only doing my job."

"Rules are rules, and I have no choice but to follow them."

"Whose stupid idea was this anyway?"

"You got us into this mess—you get us out!"

1.2 THE FOUR ESSENTIALS OF CONFLICT RESOLUTION

How can you use the four essentials of conflict to resolve a conflict? How can the four essentials of conflict become the four essentials of conflict resolution? First, consider taking a few minutes now to reflect on a past or present conflict.

- What was or is your loss (i.e., what did it cost you emotionally or tangibly)?
- What was or is the other person's intent?
- What rule or rules (e.g., boundaries) did the other person violate?
- Can the other person be held responsible for what they did?

↓ Worksheets for this exercise are available from
www.theconflictresolvingnetwork.com

There's a good chance that for this or every conflict you've ever had with anyone, all four essentials were met; that is, there was a loss, there was an intent, there was a violation, and it was clear who's to blame for what happened.

As I mentioned earlier, all four essentials depend to varying degrees on interpretation and perception, or in other words, how you both see each one. *Sometimes the perception of loss, intent, violation, or responsibility is based entirely or, to some extent, on a misunderstanding, a mistaken assumption, a mistaken expectation, or on a fact that one or both of you have gotten wrong. The reason I call loss, intent, violation, and responsibility the four essentials of conflict is because all four of them must be present for there to be a conflict. If any one of these is missing, there is either less potential for conflict or no conflict at all.*

Misunderstandings, mistaken assumptions, and unfounded expectations are all fertile ground for conflict.

What this means is that if both of you are willing to re-examine the basis of your conclusions about one another's loss, intent, violation, and responsibility, it may be possible to "knock out," nullify, or at least put in doubt, one of these essentials of conflict and in so doing nip your conflict in the bud, stop it cold, or at least de-escalate it a notch or two! Note that I'll cover this conflict resolution strategy in detail in Chapter 6.

It should also be pointed out that sometimes, even when you can conclude that there was no intent or violation behind what the other person did and that they cannot be blamed for your loss, the feeling of loss can still take some time to get over.

THE STAGES OF CONFLICT AND STEPS OF CONFLICT RESOLUTION

What's Coming Up in this Chapter...

With several key ideas covered, I'm now ready to map out for you both the stages of conflict and the steps of conflict resolution as I see them. Naturally, no two conflicts are exactly alike; and neither, for that matter, are their resolution. However, I've observed that conflicts often unfold in four stages, and that their resolution often takes place in four commonly experienced steps. The aim of this chapter is to give you a bird's eye view of these stages and steps. In Chapter 6, I'll provide you the details of what you need to know and do to navigate them successfully.

Also worth mentioning, is that just as knowing the four essentials (loss, intent, violation, and responsibility) provides you with a framework for understanding a conflict, so too does knowing the stages of a conflict and the steps of its resolution. Thinking of these stages and steps will give you more presence of mind, so you'll be better able to anticipate how things are likely to unfold and be in a better position to decide how best to handle each one. As you read this chapter, just as you may have done while reading Chapter 1, I invite you to reflect on one or more conflicts you've had in the past or on one that you are in right now.

2.1 THE FOUR STAGES OF CONFLICT

The first thing that must happen to set off a conflict is for one of you to do something that meets all four of the essentials of conflict (i.e., there's loss, there's intent, it's a violation, and someone can be held responsible). The second stage consists of some sort of response or retaliation, followed by a tit-for-tat exchange, along with the possibility of escalation. In the third stage, if escalation does take place, sooner or later it peaks and stops, and the process of de-escalation begins. The fourth, and final, stage of conflict is disengagement. Disengagement can range all the way from taking a little time apart to cool down to cutting all ties and never seeing each other again.

It's important to note that these four stages are not written in stone—not all conflicts unfold in these four stages—but many do. Furthermore, how long each stage lasts can vary considerably because any one of them can play out in a matter of minutes, hours, or days. It's also important to point out that people can, and often do, go back and forth between a couple of the stages a few times before moving on to the next one.

Stage 1: THE FOUR ESSENTIALS OF CONFLICT ARE MET

Once all four essentials are met, the potential for conflict has arisen. It's important to remember, though, this doesn't necessarily mean that a conflict will occur—it's just that the stage is set for one to happen.

Whether or not a conflict takes place depends mainly on how big you perceive your loss to be. You'll remember from Chapter 1 that loss—whether tangible or psychological—brings inequity and unfairness into your relationship. So, if your loss is great enough, you'll feel compelled to set things right in some way (e.g., respond in some way or out-and-out retaliate to get even). However, if your loss doesn't really add up to very much, or cost you that much, or mean all that much to you, you'll have little or no reason to respond in any way, let alone retaliate. So, there's no conflict.

But what if your tangible or psychological loss is big enough and you really want to get even, or at least respond in some way? Then, you must decide whether or not to do anything (at least right away). Once you've made the decision to respond in some way, and as soon as you've responded, you're in Stage 2.

Stage 2: TIT-FOR-TAT EXCHANGE AND POSSIBLE ESCALATION

In the second stage of a conflict, you might choose to respond in some restrained or measured way, choose to out-and-out retaliate, or something in-between. For example, whatever you do—and how you do it—may be proportionate to your loss, or it might not be. *In the end, the decision what to do, if anything, typically boils down to a quick cost-benefit calculation: Weighing, among other things, the pros and cons (i.e., benefits and costs)—both psychological and tangible—of responding versus the pros and cons of not responding (more about this in Chapters 5 and 6).*

The Benefits of Responding

There are some clear benefits to responding. For example, one psychological benefit is feeling good about having stood up for yourself, having gotten something off your chest or just feeling good about having gotten even. A tangible benefit might be having something of yours that was taken returned to you.

Is conflict always necessary? No, but sometimes it is. For example, sometimes the only way to stop being treated a certain way is to stand up for yourself or defend yourself, which might risk starting a conflict. Sometimes you need to clear the air to move forward in a relationship. Remember that conflict is not all bad; when successfully resolved, it can and often does strengthen relationships and build new common ground from which to move forward.

The Benefits of Not Responding

There can be benefits to not responding, though this depends on the situation. One of the key benefits of not responding is that it lessens the likelihood of escalation (which, as I'll talk about later in this chapter, can be very, very helpful). Another benefit of not responding, at least not right away, is that it can give both of you a chance to calm down. Sometimes simply disengaging pre-emptively—that is, going right to Stage 4 on your own (e.g., disengaging for a short while)—is the best thing to do.

Cooling down before you, for example, say something, send a text or an email, or even before you talk to somebody is often a really good idea. No matter how frustrated, disappointed, hurt or angry you are, sooner or later all emotions fade. Once your emotions fade enough, you'll be able to think more clearly and be more likely to come up with a measured and reasonable response rather than do something that is likely escalating.

The Costs of Not Responding

This having been said, there are also potential costs to not responding. For example, one cost of not speaking out is that if the other person doesn't know that they've done anything wrong or that something's bothering you, they'll never know unless you tell them. Furthermore, if they do know that they did something wrong, your silence will likely be seen as proof that you're OK with whatever they did, and they will likely assume they can do it again!

Another thing to remember is that not responding is a kind of response. And if you're not responding to what is obviously a provocation, let's say, then there's a chance that the other person may see it as you deliberately ignoring them, which can be infuriating for them. So, can you get escalation if you don't respond? Yes, sometimes you can.

A further cost of not doing anything is that although emotions fade, they don't always fade anywhere nearly or quickly enough; and your feelings (like anger, disappointment, and resentment) then must go somewhere. In this case, you (and possibly the other person as well) may try to gloss over what was done, explain it away, or try to either shrug it off or even laugh it off.

These coping strategies often work, but when they don't, once again, your emotions must go somewhere. Emotions do not vanish into thin air (more about this in the next chapter). At this juncture, whether you don't respond or don't retaliate because you don't want to or because you can't, you've got two options. One is to make a "withdrawal" from the "positivity account" you have with the other person; the other option is to turn your feelings inward, and put them on what I call the "emotional credit card."

Conflict and Your "Positivity Account"

You may remember in Chapter 1, I made the point that loving and liking both have the potential to reduce psychological loss, at least up to a point. Another way of putting it is to think of this as the "positivity account" you have with the other person. Your positivity account is the reservoir of love, admiration, affection or liking, along with the accumulated goodwill, respect, and trust or loyalty you feel toward someone (and ideally, the other person toward you). It can be a buffer during difficult moments in any relationship and what allows you to cut the other person (and ideally, each other) some slack.

Relationships with a long history of many happy moments together typically have a very healthy "positivity account balance." Things that help build your positivity account with someone include:

- sharing profound and intensely bonding moments together;
- sharing moments of fun, laughter, adventure, excitement and so forth;
- working together successfully on shared tasks and goals that matter a lot to both of you; and,

- having a history of sticking by one another and helping one another through thick and thin (especially during tough times).

In conflict resolution, it's often your positivity account with someone that opens the door to communication–and holds it open–when you need it most.

Conflict and Your "Emotional Credit Card"

There are situations where your positivity account with the other person has never had a chance to accumulate much of a balance or is so low that there is not much love, liking, respect or goodwill to draw upon. This means that when you experience a psychological loss because of what the other person did, that loss is covered by drawing on your "emotional credit card." This can be troublesome for two reasons:

- First, like any credit card, your emotional credit card has a limit, and, for that matter, a high interest rate—which is to say that you can't carry pent up feelings for very long. The weight of any suppressed emotion will grow ever so steadily over time, whether it's days, weeks, months, or years. And like the balance on a credit card with a high interest, that weight gets harder and harder to carry.
- The second reason why drawing on your emotional credit card with someone can be a problem is that if you must draw on it often, your credit will eventually max out. What happens when your emotional credit card maxes out? Arguments and blow ups will become more

frequent, intense, and lengthy. Indeed, people reaching the limit of their emotional credit card with someone is one of the main reasons for many relationships ending.

The psychological cost of filling up one's emotional credit card is dramatically seen among victims of bullying.

So, always remember that while responding in any conflict situation has a potential cost, so too does not responding. Now, let's return and finish up our description of the second stage of conflict.

Because every retaliation is an attempt to get even for a loss, in a tit-for-tat exchange each retaliation causes another loss to which the other person feels compelled to respond in kind. Why? Retaliating is about getting even and getting even often feels good—especially in the moment (as the saying goes, revenge is sweet). Tit-for-tat exchanges are often short-lived and quickly end in a "draw;" but they can pave the way for escalation. Why does escalation happen? There are several key reasons.

Note that these reasons apply regardless of whether the escalation occurs in-person, on a video chat, on the phone, or by text.

- One reason for escalation is that if there's pent up anger or resentment from previously unresolved conflicts with the other person to begin with, then this will add to your psychological loss and the urge to retaliate and get even.
- Another reason is that the negative feelings that make up your psychological loss can have an amplifying effect. So, if emotions become intense enough, anything the other person does will seem worse (e.g., angrier, more spiteful,

more defensive) than it likely is and so it will likely get an amplified response from you in return. What this means is that one amplified response will invite yet another equally or even more amplified response. So, you can see at this rate, it doesn't take long to reach that moment of combustion when the "gloves come off" and you've got total, all-out, escalation.

- A third reason for escalation arises when pride gets in the way. If one or both of you stubbornly won't back down because your pride (a.k.a., "ego") won't let you, then escalation is almost inevitable.

- Related to stubborn pride is refusing to listen. When people in conflict feel they are not being listened to, their voices begin to rise—which is a sure-fire escalation inducer.

- What often comes with not listening is interrupting. Saying something in the middle of whatever the other person is trying to say, making a snide or belittling comment as they're saying something that matters to them or even just making an exasperated or mocking face as they speak can be infuriating.

- One final reason for escalation worth pointing out is that escalating has become a habit that you've both fallen into.

The Potential Effects of Escalation

> "Raise your words, not your voice. It is rain that grows flowers, not thunder."
>
> RUMI (PERSIAN POET, 1207–1273)

It's because of escalation that little things can get people into big conflicts...and sometimes big trouble! Relationships can suffer a great deal of damage during escalation when, for example, by the time it has peaked the relationship is irreparably, or nearly irreparably damaged in the wake of what was done. ***Indeed, what happens during escalation can be more damaging than whatever started your conflict in the first place and can sometimes even end your relationship.***

- Escalation also increases the chance of "collateral conflict." For example, let's say you leave slamming a door behind you so hard that a cherished family heirloom falls off the shelf and breaks into pieces. "Oh! Now look what you've done!" yells your partner at the top of their lungs. So, in this case you started with one conflict, and now you have two.
- Furthermore, escalation is often polarizing; that is, it often results in both a widening apart and a hardening of both your positions. Simply put, polarization leads to both of you digging in your heels and "doubling down." ***Taken too far, polarization can turn friends into enemies.***
- Finally, and if all this wasn't bad enough, people typically have vivid and lasting memories of what was said and done during escalation—things that are sometimes hard to forgive, and impossible to forget.

If I were ever visited by the Fairy Godmother of conflict resolution and granted just one wish, it would be this: That anyone who has not yet done so, learn one of the most important conflict resolution skills I can think of; namely, the ability to catch-and stop-yourself escalating (especially if it's become a habit).

The reason? If all else fails, being able to stop an escalation guarantees a "softer landing" to any conflict, which lessens the negative impact of whatever the conflict is about and renders it far less damaging to everyone involved.

If the two of you see how much damage escalation can do to your relationship, then, if you can, agree on a word or phrase, or some signal that means LET'S STOP THIS ESCALATION RIGHT NOW BEFORE IT GOES TOO FAR!

Always consider calling a truce! If you can catch yourself escalating, one very helpful thing you can do then is call a truce. A truce is basically a ceasefire; that is, an agreement between you and the other person to stop arguing or fighting, at least for a while. So rather than continuing to escalate, you both make a conscious effort to let your emotions settle and give yourselves some time to decide what to do. While truces can certainly be fragile and tensions can remain high, one of the nice things about a truce is that, compared to escalating, the door is open to offering an olive branch, which is the first step of the conflict resolution process.

All this having been said, it's important to point out that escalation isn't always just thunder, lightning, and fury. Sometimes you simply must clear the air with someone. This can be both cleansing and helpful—especially when there are grievances and frustrations on both sides that both of you need to tell one another about.

Furthermore, sometimes during escalation people say important things to one another—things that they may have bottled up for a long time. To be sure, doing so risks sparking an escalation, or fueling one that's already started, but sometimes it can actually stop an escalation dead in its tracks. Why? Because sometimes what is finally said suddenly shines a spotlight on what the conflict is **really** about; that is to say, the conflict behind the conflict. When this happens, whatever elephant may have been in the room can no longer be ignored.

Stage 3: DE-ESCALATION

There is often an element of "brinksmanship" to escalation, but sooner or later, escalation reaches a peak, stops, and de-escalation follows. Why does escalation peak and prompt de-escalation? There are a few possible reasons; for example:

- one of you thinks "We're even now!" and the other also thinks "Yeah, we're even" and neither of you escalates any further;
- one or both of you have sufficiently vented, spent your anger and other feelings, or gotten what you wanted to say off your chest; or,
- both of you realize that the benefit or risk of further escalation isn't worth it (e.g., "I don't want to say something I might regret later...").

De-escalation can also be motivated by "conflict fatigue." Conflict fatigue can set in when one or both of you have tired yourselves out—or are exhausted from—the escalation. You're both so emotionally drained and exhausted from the fight that neither of you want to continue.

Alternatively, conflict fatigue often hits you when you realize that you've gone round and round in circles, and that after all your effort, you're right back to where you started. Finally, conflict fatigue can stem from having gotten sick and tired not just of the fight you're having now, but of all the fights you've been having.

Conflict fatigue can drive you further apart and prompt one of you to throw up your hands in exasperation and say something like:

"I give up."
"OK, fine—you win!"
"OK, you're right."
"Whatever...." (this word, all by itself, can set off another escalation!)

Giving up and giving in may end a conflict but ending a conflict and resolving it are not the same thing. Neither giving up nor giving in are the same thing as resolving!

On a more positive note, conflict fatigue can also compel both of you to try to de-escalate and make peace. Whatever the reason for de-escalating, once one of you begins to tone down your reaction, and if the other person follows suit, you'll have de-escalation and an easing of tensions. De-escalation is a calming-down period, and it can also stop or lessen any polarization that's occurred. It's in the de-escalation stage, that we sometimes see a spontaneous apology or peace offering made by one or both people.

It is possible to have re-escalation followed again by de-escalation—even a few times—before you are both finally ready to de-escalate.

Stage 4: DISENGAGEMENT

Either during escalation—or even after de-escalation—one or both of you may feel a strong urge to withdraw, distance yourselves or disengage emotionally as well as physically from one another. If so, you might hear yourself saying something like:

> "I need to be alone."
> "I've had it!"
> "I can't take this anymore—I'm outta here!"
> "I'm done!"
> "We're done!"

Disengagement is not a forgone ending to every conflict.
As noted above, if during de-escalation an apology or peace
offering is made and accepted, the process of resolution
might start right there and then.

When people disengage, it's often to escape the stress of the conflict and prevent it from going any further. Disengagement can also stem from deciding that there's no point in trying to resolve the conflict, at least for now. It might be worth trying to resolve later, or maybe not (e.g., if you decide there's no point in carrying on with the relationship).

Disengagement can last a few minutes or a few hours (e.g., one or both of you just need some "space" to cool down). Disengagement can also last a few days or weeks, or a few months (e.g., a trial separation). Of course, disengagement can also be permanent. In fact, permanently disengaging is often used as the simplest way of ending a relationship (e.g., walking out and never coming back; ghosting). Permanent disengagement is not always the best solution, but sometimes, it's by no means the worst; and in some cases, it is the best option for you as well as everyone else involved.

Short-term emotional disengagement is normal and can be helpful
and healthy. However, long-term emotional disengagement on the
part of one or both of you does not bode well.

> "Solitude is a good place to visit but a
> poor place to stay."
> JOSH BILLINGS [HENRY WHEELER SHAW]
> (AMERICAN HUMORIST, 1818–1885)

Feelings can change during disengagement. For example, early on in disengagement you might be angry at someone, but as your anger fades, your feelings of fondness or affection for that person, if you had them in the first place, gradually re-emerge. If or when this happens, disengagement often becomes an opportunity to begin to weigh the plusses and minuses of resolving your conflict and begin to think about the ins and outs of what this may involve. I'll talk more about this in Chapter 5.

During the disengagement stage—and many people do this— you might "replay" the conflict in your mind and imagine how it could have gone differently. You may also conclude that, for example, you're "better off," that you "deserve better," "could do better," that "it's just not worth it," or that you "just don't care anymore." Of course, at the same time, the other person may well be thinking or trying to convince themselves of exactly the same thing about you.

If any of these things are true for both of you then your disengagement is likely to be complete and permanent (at least if it's possible to walk away from the relationship and never see the other person again). If on the other hand, neither of you are fully convinced of any of these sorts of things, then sooner or later during this stage one or both of you might:

- begin to re-think your perceptions and conclusions about one another's loss, intent, violation, and responsibility;
- look back on your points of disagreement and begin to see them in a different light and perhaps see some merit in the other person's point of view; or,
- start to miss each other enough, or at least some things about one another enough, to consider sending a signal or message to see if the other person would like to re-engage. One or both of you may even reach out to offer some token of goodwill, or a sign of peace, or an "olive branch."

Two additional points about the disengagement stage—whether emotional or both physical and emotional—are noteworthy: During this stage, some people must reconnect at least once to deal with some practical matter, which may or may not have some bearing on the eventual outcome of this stage. Second, people sometimes choose to just partially disengage. Sometimes it's easier that way. Sometimes it's because ending the relationship by cutting all ties and never seeing the person again is not an option.

Partial disengagement may mean just cutting back on the amount of time you spend together, texting or chatting less often, or rearranging your relationship in some way. For example, by taking one or more items off your relationship menu (i.e., the things you talk about, or do together or do for one another), at least for a while.

One particularly problematic form of disengagement worth warning you about is being in what might be called *relationship limbo*. More than just refusing to speak to one another, or when someone gets the "silent treatment" for a while, relationship limbo is when two people (in my experience, it's often been family members) disengage by refusing to speak to one another for months or even years.

There can be many reasons why relationship limbo can happen, but one thing is for sure: When you're not on speaking terms, you're not communicating, and without communication, conflicts can continue indefinitely. *In fact, the one thing that conflict thrives on as much as miscommunication, is when there's no communication.*

Preemptive Disengagement

Some people, at the first sign of conflict, opt to skip the tit-for-tat exchange of Stage 2, and jump to disengagement right away. Preemptive disengagement is by no means a bad thing; for example, walking away from a potential conflict (e.g., someone taunting you) is sometimes the smartest and bravest thing you can do. Similarly, preemptively disengaging for as long as you need to cool down and prevent escalation is also a good thing.

Sometimes people preemptively disengage if they are so fed up with the conflict (and the other person) that they'd rather disengage than endure what they see as another pointless quarrel with no hope of resolution. In this case, preemptive disengagement may mean deciding that they've had enough and want to end the relationship—that is, disengage permanently. Sometimes people preemptively disengage because they see no point in trying to resolve the conflict because, even if they do, it is bound to arise again, as it has done so many times in the past.

Calling a Truce vs. Disengaging

As with escalation, an alternative to preemptively or fully disengaging, is to call a truce. And as with calling a truce to stop escalation, when you call a truce instead of disengaging, the door is open a little wider and it's a little more inviting to the offering of an olive branch.

Take a few minutes now to reflect on past conflicts you've had. Did they unfold in these four steps? Did any of them involve calling a truce?

Worksheets for this exercise are available from
www.theconflictresolvingnetwork.com

2.2 THE FOUR STEPS OF CONFLICT RESOLUTION

Just as conflict often unfolds in four stages, conflict resolution often takes place in four steps. The first step is when one person makes the first move and, ideally along with it, gives a sign of peace or offers an "olive branch." The second step, which I call conflict "unpacking," involves clarifying any misperceptions, misinterpretations, or misunderstandings that may have led to the conflict in the first place and, along with that, identifying any point(s) of disagreement that stand in the way of resolving it. It is these points of disagreement, or sticking points, that you then take to the third step. The third step involves resolving any disagreements or sticking points as far as you both can, and if need be, coming up with new rules and roles for the relationship that you can both abide by (i.e., rearranging your relationship). The fourth and final step is reconciling and, when you can, celebrating the successful resolution of your conflict in some way.

As with the stages of conflict, it's important to note that not all conflicts are resolved in these four steps, but many are, and that the time each step takes can vary, depending on the nature of the conflict and the people involved. I will go into fuller detail on navigating these four stages in Chapter 6.

Step 1: OFFERING AN OLIVE BRANCH

> *"It takes two to quarrel,*
> *but only one to end it."*
> **SPANISH PROVERB**

While every step in the conflict resolution process is critical, the olive branch offering is perhaps the most critical because nothing happens without it. Simply put, one of you must make the first move. Offering a token of goodwill or a peace offering (i.e., an olive branch), signals your decision to make that first move. It could be a text, an email, a phone call, or a bouquet of flowers, all depending on the kind of relationship you have and the nature of the conflict you're in.

Your olive branch may not get accepted at first if it requires a "sweetening" of your offer. So, during this stage there may be some back-and-forth between the two of you (and a kind of "olive branch dance" begins). Sooner or later, the other person accepts your offer, or says "I'll think about it..." or rejects it outright (in which case, there would be a return to disengagement, which may or may not be permanent).

Note that apologies are often offered–and accepted–during this step, but apologies can be offered at any step in the resolution of a conflict.

Step 2: CONFLICT UNPACKING

> *"What is in the way, is the way."*
> LAO-TZU, (CHINESE PHILOSOPHER, 604–531 B.C.)

It is hard to get to the bottom of a conflict when you're in the middle of it. So, it's only when you're both ready that the two of you can move on to the second step of the conflict resolution process. Whereas the goal of Step 1 is to get the two of you out of disengagement (and at least on texting or speaking terms), the main goal of Step 2 is to sort out (i.e., "unpack") what happened so that, hopefully, you never have this conflict happen again.

To accomplish this, you need to communicate. Why? Because conflict resolution needs clarity, and clarity needs awareness of what both of you are thinking and feeling. But for both awareness and clarity to help you in a conflict, you need to communicate openly with one another. ***Simply put, the best place to start in conflict resolution is with clarity, and clarity needs communication.***

So, there are four key things you need to try to do in Step 2. First, give yourselves the chance to tell one another what happened from your points of view. Second, give yourselves the chance to tell one another how you feel about what the other person did that triggered a tangible or psychological loss for you (the exercises in the next chapter will help with this).

The third aim of Step 2 is to give both of you the chance to bring your point of view and ideas forward to see if, together, you can come to a new understanding of what happened. The idea is to thereby try to clear up any misperceptions, misinterpretations, or misunderstandings that may have led to the conflict in the first place. Simply put, in this step both of you take some time together to figure out what went wrong and try to solve the problem that sparked your conflict. Successfully unpacking and solving problems together not only strengthens your relationship, but it can also be trajectory-changing—that is, it can change where and how far your relationship may go. More about this later in the chapter.

To unpack and problem-solve, you can use the four essentials. You'll remember from Chapter 1 that all four essentials must be present for there to be a conflict and that sometimes the perception of loss, intent, violation, or responsibility is based on a misunderstanding. So, if you're both willing to re-think your conclusions about one another's loss, intent, violation, and responsibility, you might be able to resolve your conflict right there and then. If not, it's likely because there is something that you still don't agree on which may have either helped start the conflict in the first place, or is keeping it going. So, the fourth, and final, purpose of this step is to identify any points of disagreement you still may have, and to take those to Step 3.

Step 3: DISAGREEMENT RESOLUTION

It is important to distinguish between the conflict you are having with someone and the disagreement over which you are having the conflict. If you've ever heard the phrase "let's agree to disagree," you'll recognize the value of making the distinction between the conflict you have with someone, and the disagreement over which you are having the conflict (which some writers refer to as the dispute).

Conflict will almost always involve one or more points of disagreement that have helped spark the conflict in the first place, or have a hand in keeping it going. *While the dispute is what you disagree on with the other person, what generates conflict is the emotion that arises over what you're disagreeing on.*

You know you're in a serious conflict with someone if, when you disagree over something, the things you say to one another are more damaging to your relationship than whatever it was you disagreed on.

You also know you're in a serious conflict when, time after time, progressively more anger than understanding–i.e., more "heat than light"–gets generated when the two of you argue. If you've ever been in an argument so heated that at some point you've both forgotten what it was that started it, or what you were arguing about, then you'll know exactly what I'm talking about.

The goal of Step 3 is to come up with solutions to any disagreements or sticking points that were not resolved in Step 2 as best as you both can. In taking this step, both of you might be able to see each other's points of disagreement in a different light and perhaps also see some merit in each other's point of view, whether they are about the facts of the matter, each person's side of the story, or differences in values. It might also end in having to agree to disagree. You may also, as a means of coming to a solution, rearrange some aspects of your relationship to make it work better for both of you. Dealing with disagreements and value conflicts, as well as rearranging relationships are covered in detail in Chapter 6.

Step 4: RECONCILIATION AND CELEBRATION

At this point, your conflict is in the rearview mirror. Resolving a conflict and reconciling—that is, returning to a state of peace between the two of you—can be transformative for your relationship and, if you can, should be celebrated in some way. What you do to celebrate varies on the nature of your relationship, but whatever it is, it can, in some cases, mark a new beginning.

Moments of reconciliation and celebration after a conflict can add a lot to your positivity account with the other person. In beautiful moments like this bad feelings can be completely dissolved.

Consider taking a few minutes now to reflect on past conflicts you've resolved. Did their resolution follow these four steps?

Worksheets for this exercise are available from
www.theconflictresolvingnetwork.com

2.3 SOME HELPFUL THINGS TO BEAR IN MIND GOING FORWARD

All Relationships Have Trajectories that Potentially Can be Changed for the Better

With every successful resolution of a conflict, you change where and how far any relationship you have with someone might go— regardless of the kind of relationship it is. In other words, you change both its outlook and its potential. Even a small change in the way you relate to one another now can lead to progressively more significant and lasting change in your relationship and, over time, make a difference as to where it goes.

The principle of trajectory works because every time you successfully resolve a conflict (big or small), new options open up for what's on your "relationship menu" (i.e., the things you talk about and the things you do together and for one another) now and in the future. These new options and the choices you make in the way you relate to one another, can lead to yet more options emerging which have the effect, over time, of gradually moving your relationship away from the downward trend it could have taken.

OK, so let's say you've either resolved a conflict with someone, nipped one in the bud or prevented one from happening altogether; it could have been a conflict with your spouse, partner, child, or best friend... whomever. This, of course, is terrific, and the bonus is this: Although they may be subtle at first, the effects of any positive change you make in any relationship can accumulate over time. So, the earlier any conflict is resolved, the better!

The Trajectory Principle

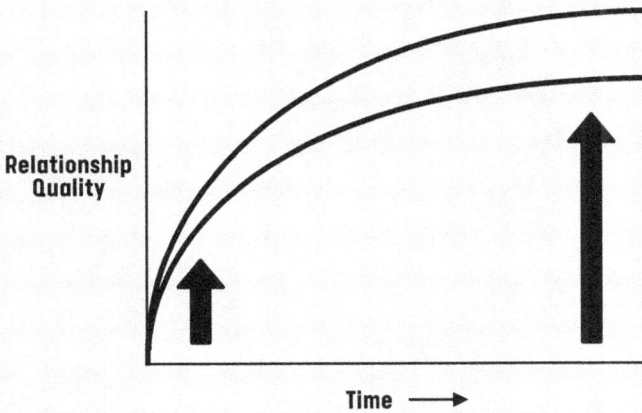

Every small positive change in a relationship now can have a significant impact on the quality of that relationship months and even years from now.

Some of the most commonly heard phrases when people try to resolve a conflict are: "Why didn't you say something?," Why didn't you tell me?," and Why didn't you tell me sooner?"

There's one additional thing to mention about trajectory: It only looks smooth when you zoom out far enough over a long enough time. If you look closely, say over days, or weeks or even months, you see lots of ups and downs. When you look at a good relationship over any number of years, most of the ups and downs get smoothed out. There is always more bumpiness in the short term than there is in the long term, which reflects the ebb and flow of any relationship.

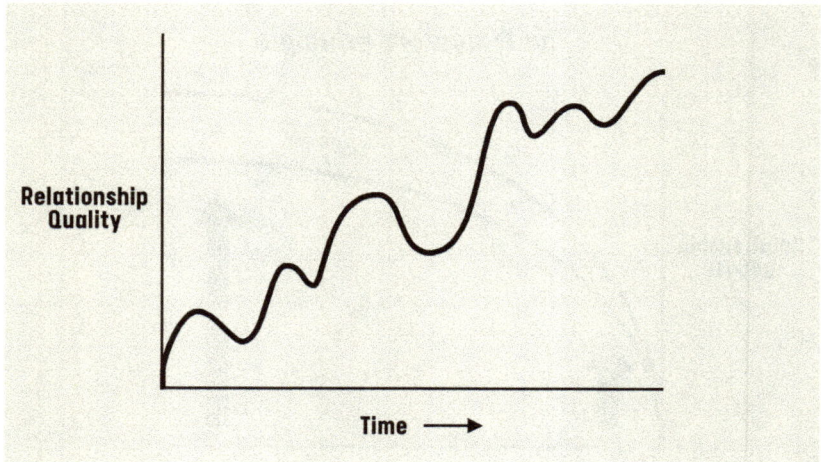

Here are some points to keep in mind the next time you hit a bump on the road in your relationship with someone:

- All relationships have ups and downs but when you're in conflict, it's much easier to remember and focus on the downs than on the ups you've had together. Try not to be too swayed by this. Memory tends to be selective.
- Big setbacks can be hard to recover from for many reasons but one of them is that the falls in any relationship are often steep and fast, while getting back to where you were can take a long time (and a lot of effort).
- This having been said, it's a really good sign when, every time you resolve a conflict, your relationship not only rebounds, but rebounds to a higher level of trust and connection than ever before. Note too, that the time it takes for your relationship to rebound or recover from a setback is an excellent indicator of its resilience.
- Never forget that every successful resolution of a conflict—no matter how small—helps build a stronger and healthier relationship—no matter what kind of relationship it is.

The Three Basic Types of Conflict: Transitory, Structural and Foundational

1. Transitory Conflict

Transitory conflict is generally the least serious and shortest-lasting of the three—often requiring you and the other person to make minor, if any, adjustments to your relationship. Transitory conflicts are like "relationship bloopers"—they tend to be "one-offs" that are not linked to one another in any way. They are rarely, if ever, repeated, and are easily forgiven and forgotten. *Transitory conflicts are commonly experienced early on in relationships when people are just getting to know one another.*

2. Structural Conflict

Most significant conflicts are of this type. The presence of a structural conflict is often signaled by frequent disagreements, arguments, fights, or all-out blow ups. When conflicts have gradually increased in how often they occur, how intense they are and how long they last, this often is a sign that there is a deeper, underlying conflict going on; that is to say, a conflict behind the conflict.

At the very least, it could suggest that one or more aspects of the relationship are out of balance. Consequently, both people may have to consider rearranging their relationship (including sometimes its nature, scope, or purpose) for it to work. Rearranging means changing or adjusting one or more aspects of your relationship; for example, the way you relate to one another, the rules of your relationship, and what's on your relationship menu. Needless to say, the extent of rearrangement required varies considerably from relationship to relationship and from situation to situation. Rearranging relationships is covered in Chapter 6.

If something looks like a transitory conflict at first, can it turn out to be structural? Yes. It sometimes takes time for a pattern to emerge, which may then point to a deeper conflict. Sometimes the surface reasons for disagreements, arguments, fights, and so forth are one thing, and the real or deeper reasons are another.

3. *Foundational Conflict*

Foundational conflict is, by definition, deeply entrenched, and sometimes so long-standing that neither person can remember when it started, or, in some cases, even why it started, how it started, or who started it. Foundationally conflicted relationships typically contain fundamental incompatibilities; for example, two clashing personalities, two people with goals that are forever opposed to one another or two people who have irreconcilable values, beliefs and attitudes that make seeing eye-to-eye on almost anything nearly impossible.

Sadly, some people are in foundational conflict and there is no easy way out (e.g., a workplace conflict in which the only way out is to quit a job that one cannot afford to quit). *Indeed, one of the most difficult things for anyone is to be in a relationship they need more than they want.*

Just as it's hard to fix the foundation of a house, foundational conflicts are hard to resolve. Typically, relationships in foundational conflict cycle from one quarrel or fight to some degree of resolution for a while and then sooner or later right back to yet another quarrel or fight, over and over again, indefinitely. What foundational conflict looks like is this:

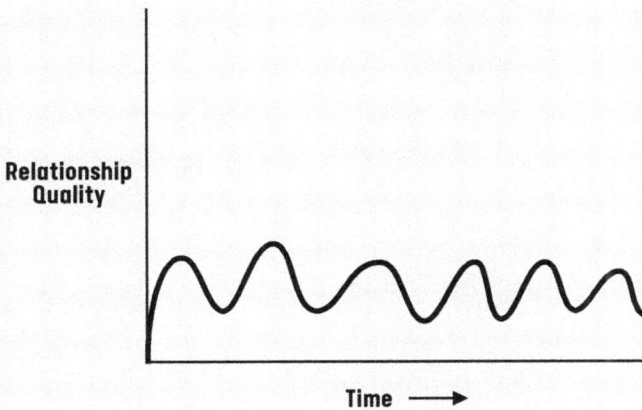

Note that in a foundational conflict the relationship has ups and downs but with no climb in its quality. By contrast, in a healthy relationship there are ups and downs but with a slow and steady climb in quality.

Can something that looks like a structural conflict at first turn out to be foundational? Yes. If repeated attempts at resolution and relationship rearranging with different adjustments don't work, it's likely that the nature of the conflict is foundational.

As challenging as structural and foundational conflicts can both be, as I said in the preface to this book, the quality of any relationship depends not on the absence of conflict, but on how well the two of you resolve it when it does arise. Always remember that while it is true that sometimes conflict can bring out the worst in us, its successful resolution has the potential to bring out the best.

WHEN IN CONFLICT
EMOTION POWERS, THINKING GUIDES

What's Coming Up in this Chapter...

When in conflict, your emotions can often "hijack" your thinking and leave you lost for words or cause you to choose words that you regret later (which is why even the smartest people can sometimes say—and do—the dumbest things...). Plainly speaking, ***conflict is primarily felt, not thought,*** which is one of the reasons I wrote this chapter and why I think it will be helpful to you.

Even though conflict is primarily felt rather than thought, thoughts and feelings go together; you can't have one without the other, like yin and yang or peanut butter and jam.... While thoughts and words live in our minds, our feelings are felt all throughout our bodies. This is what makes emotions so powerful and what makes them "stick around" long after the moment has passed. For their part, thoughts and words can influence what we feel in the first place, as well as how we express in words what it is we feel. What this means is that understanding the dynamics of thoughts and feelings—the topic of this chapter—is central because saying how you feel and why is essential to resolving most conflicts.

3.1 EMOTION POWERS, THINKING GUIDES

Most people don't give this much thought, but the two things that occupy pretty much every moment of your waking life are your thoughts and your feelings. Thoughts are made up of your ongoing, continuous stream of inner conversation, commentary, and observation. Sometimes, thoughts take the form of words and at other times they seem wordless. Sometimes thoughts are concentrated and purposeful; and sometimes they are erratic and rambling. At times, thoughts come effortlessly and at other times it takes hard work for them to become clear.

Whatever content and form they take, your thoughts and feelings influence one another back and forth constantly; indeed, they are so interwoven that it is often hard for you to know when a thought ends and a feeling begins, or when a feeling begins and a thought ends.

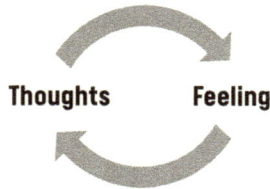

Thoughts   Feeling

As entwined as they are, thinking and feeling are very different in both their nature and function in your life. One way to think of the difference is this: ***Emotion powers, thinking guides.*** To illustrate, imagine yourself in a sailboat, gently bobbing up and down in the middle of a placid lake on a sunny, cloudless day. Feelings are like the wind that must fill your sail for you to move, and thoughts are like the rudder you steer with. With only the wind, you have no control over where you go, and with only a rudder, you go nowhere. You need both.

Now, just as a sailboat needs wind to move, consider this: Without feelings, would you be moved to do anything? Without longing, passion, or desire, would you ever fall in love with anyone? Or for that matter, be passionate about anything? Would you want to protect those who love and depend on you from harm? Be a friend to anyone? Could you ever experience joy or share a laugh with anyone? Without hopes, dreams or ambition, would you ever strive to accomplish anything? Without confidence, would you ever even try?

3.2 THE POWER OF EMOTION

To get a feel (no pun intended) for the power of emotion, I'd like you to picture a glass of water. Now, picture a single drop of ink hitting the water. In the twinkling of an eye, this drop billows out in all directions at once and colors the water throughout. Like that drop of ink, a feeling can spread into every nook and cranny of your mind in a split second.

So, not only can a feeling come upon you in an instant, whether you're happy or sad, angry or calm, embarrassed or beaming with pride, but it can also color not only what you see, but what and how, you think about what you see.

**Everybody knows it's hard to think "outside the box;"
well, it's even harder to think outside the mood!**

The Qualities that Give Feelings their Power

Of the many qualities that give feelings their power, there are several that are especially important to bear in mind.

- You experience feelings in places all over your body, which makes emotions hard for you to ignore; on top of which, never forget that when it comes to emotions, your body doesn't lie (either your heart leaps when you see someone, or it doesn't). You can try, but sooner or later, as I pointed out in Chapter 2, emotions must go somewhere—they can only be pent up for so long.

One of the reasons that expressing pent-up feelings feels so good is that doing so relieves the tension that comes from holding them back, and that relief in itself–on top of everything else–feels good.

- When negative feelings build up about someone, the relationship can increasingly feel like a burden. Fatigue may set in, and there is the chance that sooner or later there will come a point when the weight of this burden is too much to bear, as when the proverbial straw breaks the camel's back.
- In contrast, with positive feelings about someone, you never feel heavy or weighed down. Quite the opposite: You feel buoyed, lightened, and uplifted.
- While a single thought may come and go in a second, feelings sometimes take a long time to fade. Note that although the fading of an emotion is one thing, forgetting how you felt is quite another: A strong feeling might take a day or two to fade, but it may take years to forget how you felt.
- Compared to remembering facts and figures, when you recall how you felt with someone, you often don't remember many details. People often say: "I don't remember exactly what happened or what was said, but I remember how I felt."
- Feelings toward someone can change over time; for example, fun with someone can turn into affection and

affection can turn into love. On the flip side, disappointment can turn into sadness, sadness into hurt, and hurt into anger. A change of heart can happen in a matter of minutes, hours, or days; although sometimes (as when people drift apart) it happens over the course of months or years.

- You can be influenced by feelings you have about someone but wish you didn't. These are the sorts of feelings that you're not willing or able to fully admit to having (either to yourself or anyone else), that you fight, try to push away, or deny.

- You can also be influenced by feelings toward someone that lurk below the surface of your everyday awareness. Feelings like this can pop up when you're with that person (or when you're thinking of them) in the most unexpected—and sometimes awkward—ways. If you've ever made a Freudian slip, you'll know exactly what I'm talking about...

So, Are Feelings Irrational?

Do all these points about the power of emotion mean that feelings are irrational? Many people think so; for example, when they say: "My rational side says... but my emotional side says...". But thinking and feeling are not opposites; they are simply different. *Feelings are neither rational nor irrational—it's only the thought, or reason, behind a feeling, that can be rational or irrational.*

I'm sure you can relate to this point if you've ever looked back on something you did once and asked yourself, "What on earth was I thinking!?"

Anger

As you may remember from Chapter 1, loss occurs when someone takes something of value from you or short-changes you; or when someone does something to you that you don't want done to you; or, when someone withholds or refuses or neglects to give you something that you do want, expect, or believe is owed you. How do you feel when this happens? Well, it likely depends on the nature of your relationship with that person and the nature and magnitude of your loss. However, the single, most common, and sometimes first and strongest emotion that people feel in conflict, is anger.

Sometimes, the first thing people feel isn't anger. Sometimes it's shock, dismay, hurt, and even fear. But when these emotions fade what often bubbles up is anger.

I'm sometimes asked: Isn't it wrong to be angry? Not necessarily—it all depends. First, anger can be healthy, have a useful purpose and play a positive role by—like any emotion—"powering" you in a positive way. For example, by helping you to:

- mobilize your resources
- galvanize your resolve
- stand up for yourself, speak out and assert your rights, and
- stand up to manipulation or intimidation.

Furthermore, expressing your anger in the right way and at the right time can and often does lead to positive outcomes, such as clearing the air, forming a better relationship, and feeling better about yourself. On top of all this, expressing anger in the right way and at the right time often gets good things said and done that would not otherwise have happened.

Second, anger sends an immediate signal to the other person that something's wrong—even if it's just a furrowed brow or a glaring look in your eyes. It can tell the other person that there is something serious going on and that whatever is bothering you should not be treated lightly.

Anger is often the first signal that you send to the other person, or the other person sends to you, that says something's not right. If you ever get such a signal—and you're not sure what it means or why—always ask: "Is there something wrong?" "Are you mad at me?" or "Have I said or done something to upset you?" *If you're not sure why, always clarify!*

OK, so when is anger a problem? Anger is problematic if, as with any emotion, the reason for it is on shaky grounds to begin with. Anger can also be problematic if its intensity, or the way you express it, is out of proportion with your reason for being angry. For example, anger can become especially toxic to you when it turns spiteful, vindictive, malicious, or hateful.

Anger can also become a problem when you either take it out on a scapegoat or turn it inward and charge it to your emotional credit card, or when it has become your "go to" response and it has gotten easier and easier to get angry over less and less, and escalation has become a habit. Finally, anger is a problem when it shuts both of you down and cuts off all communication.

Any one of these situations may signal that the anger you're feeling is just the tip of an iceberg and that there are some deeper issues that ought to be resolved (e.g., anger and resentment over something that happened a long time ago). Feeling angry much of the time, or simply having a "short fuse"—being easily frustrated or angered—can also come from having a long-standing structural, or even foundational conflict with someone, with all its grudges and resentments spilling over into many other situations and dealings with other people.

Anger and Passive Aggression

Anger sometimes leads to aggression. Why? Because aggression is a way of delivering a loss (tangible or psychological) to get even for the loss you've suffered. Simply put, aggression is one way of getting even.

Of course, anger doesn't always end in someone acting on it; but when it does, it can take on one of two forms: Passive or active. Active aggression means out-and-out, face-to-face hostility toward the person you're angry at (e.g., swearing at them or insulting them to their face). Passive aggression expresses anger indirectly. Passive aggression can take many forms; for example, spreading gossip or rumors, openly commenting and complaining about someone's shortcomings to other people—even strangers (e.g., "Thank you, Sir, for holding the door open for me—my partner would never think of doing that."), secretly sabotaging someone's efforts, withholding what someone wants (and making up some lie to rationalize or try to excuse it), making snide remarks that are explained away as "just kidding", teasing that's mean-spirited rather than friendly and light-hearted, giving someone the silent treatment, and so forth.

Spiteful and malicious anger is often expressed through passive aggression.

3.3 THE HELPFUL QUALITIES OF THINKING

As powerful as feelings are, they are not all-powerful. Although it's true that sometimes a feeling can come over you without you knowing exactly why, there's often a thought behind it. What does this mean? It means that thinking can either be helpful or unhelpful. For example, a single thought can prompt you to start a conflict or stop one, escalate a conflict or de-escalate it—all depending on what it is you're thinking. So, if emotions power and thinking guides, how can thinking help guide conflict resolution?

- It's thinking that gives you words that are essential to communication. In fact, it's often when we can't put our feelings into words in a conflict that we get frustrated, and things get worse (the exercise coming up in Section 3.7 can help with this).
- Emotions cannot figure themselves out, you need thinking for that. While it's true that a lot of the time your feelings can't be or don't need to be figured out, when trying to resolve a conflict, they often do.
- It's thinking that can get you out of a funk and, for example, see the brighter side of things.
- You can use thinking to re-think your assumptions, perceptions, and conclusions around the four essentials and clear up any misperceptions, misinterpretations, or misunderstandings that one or both of you have.
- Thinking is what enables you to work through your points of disagreement and stay on track during those— often tough and sometimes awkward—conversations you'll have at the second and third steps of the conflict resolution process.
- Thinking is what helps you see when the other person has a good point, and that, no matter how angry or irritated you may be by it, you can see some truth in what they said.
- Similarly, you can also use thinking to consider the other person's point of view and come up with more than one solution for resolving your conflict.
- Thinking is also what enables you to weigh your options and to decide what is really important and helpful for you to pay attention to—and what is not.

- Finally, thinking can help you come to terms with whatever the outcome of trying to resolve a conflict is and learn from it.

3.4 THE QUALITIES OF THINKING THAT CAN MAKE IT UNHELPFUL

While it's true that thinking can guide us in conflict resolution, can it ever misguide us? Yes, it can. First, we all have blind spots: We don't see things perfectly because ***perception is not just what you see, it is also what you think about what you see.***

You can have 20:20 vision, but no one has 20:20 perception.

Second, we've all got soft spots and biases. Our thinking is never perfect—it's subject to its own errors and can certainly play tricks on us. For example:

- We sometimes overthink things and end up reading meaning into situations when there isn't that much meaning there at all.

It's easy to _misread_ between the lines.

- Sometimes we ruminate about a conflict and mistake it for thinking. When you're thinking about a conflict, you're reflecting on what happened from different angles. Rumination is looking at what happened from the same angle, over and over again.

When you're ruminating, you end up spending a lot of time with the same thought about the situation going around and around in your head. Not only is rumination draining, but it rarely sheds any new light on what you're ruminating about. In fact, it's quite the opposite: Rumination is the perfect breeding ground for what I call "inner escalation."

Beware of Inner Escalation!

- Inner escalation occurs when you get more and more wound up thinking the same thought (or variations of it) about someone you're in conflict with. In inner escalation, your thinking takes various unhelpful forms, for example:
  - replaying the one or more conflicts you had with someone (and feeling like you're reliving them every time);
  - thinking about what you would have, could have, or should have done the last time you had a run-in with that person; and,
  - imagining the next run-in or some other conflict (which usually has a more and more dire ending with each go around).

With inner escalation it doesn't take long to start imagining all kinds of terrible outcomes and get yourself very worked up.

> *"I am an old man and have known a great many troubles, but most of them have never happened."*
> MARK TWAIN (1835–1910)

3.5 EMOTIONAL TRIGGERS

You may be thinking: "OK, I get it. How I think about a situation will influence how I feel about it. So, depending on what I make of what I see, I might, for example, get angry. But there are some situations when thinking doesn't even seem to come into play—'boom!'—I feel something right away. Why is that?" People often ask me this sort of question, and the answer typically lies in how emotional triggers work.

The idea that we all have triggers or "buttons" (as some people like to call them), has been around a long time and is very helpful in understanding emotions. Although feelings can seem to come out of the blue, they never actually do—feelings are always triggered by something.

In everyday use, the phrase "emotional trigger" has come to refer to things that evoke negative feelings. But many things can and do trigger positive feelings; for example, reminders of happy times can certainly "press" some very pleasant buttons, not to mention the sight of a scampering puppy or a smiling baby, or the warmth of an embrace, or hearing words of sincere thanks and appreciation! So, I see two kinds of emotional triggers, which I have dubbed "flashpoints" and "fireworks." Emotional flashpoints trigger negative feelings, and emotional fireworks trigger positive ones.

Flashpoint Triggers and Firework Triggers

Flashpoint triggers are persons, places, things, or situations that become linked to unpleasant events in your life; that is, things that were sad, hurtful, frightening, overwhelming or traumatic. Flashpoint triggers evoke memories—sometimes very vivid ones—and strong emotions. Many of our deepest flashpoint triggers, or simply flashpoints, are basically potent reminders of the worst things that have happened to us, or that we have seen happen to others.

Other flashpoints include persons, places, things, or situations that remind you of things about yourself or your life that you intensely dislike or wish you could change. Flashpoint triggers can also be reminders of specific things you dislike about someone else, or what it is you don't like about some people, or the things they do. In any event, whatever your flashpoint triggers are, they consistently hit a raw nerve and can trigger all sorts of feelings like anger, hurt, sadness, resentment, exasperation, or revulsion. I'm sure you can think of a few of your top flashpoints now.

Firework triggers are the opposite of flashpoints. Your fireworks are the persons, places, things, or situations that remind you of pleasant and joyful events in your life. Your firework triggers, or simply fireworks, evoke feelings of excitement, peace, happiness, pleasure, joy, delight, and contentment. *Your deepest fireworks bring you the moments that you live for and make whatever it took to get to these moments worthwhile.* As with your flashpoints, I'm sure you can think of some of your top fireworks now.

The specific things that can trigger emotions–whether positive or negative–can take many forms, like any reminder: Sounds (e.g., a song, a melody, the sound of someone's voice), sights (including symbols, like a flag), touch, and smells (which can be especially potent reminders).

Certain thoughts can be flashpoint triggers, such as when you think about unfairness, inequity, prejudice, hypocrisy, rejection, failure, or abandonment. Firework thoughts can be about things like belonging, kindness, redemption, and acceptance. Even feelings themselves can be potent reminders and therefore trigger other feelings (which is why, as hard as it is to think outside the box, it's just as hard–or harder–to think outside the mood!).

Before moving on, there are a few things worth bearing in mind about flashpoints or fireworks:

- We've all got them, although not everybody's got the same ones.
- People differ quite a lot in how big a flashpoint or a firework is for them; for example, what's just a pet peeve for you can be a major flashpoint for someone else, or vice versa.
- If you've ever gone grocery shopping while hungry, it's likely that all sorts of things caught your eye that you wouldn't ordinarily consider buying. Some of them even seemed to jump off the shelves at you. Your flashpoints and fireworks are like just that—they easily grab your attention.
- Your biggest flashpoints and fireworks can stop you dead in your tracks, make the hairs on the back of your neck stand up, send shivers down your spine, give you goosebumps, put a lump in your throat, bring you a sudden surge of joy (or rage), make your eyes light up, or bring tears to them.
- You usually know exactly where your fireworks and flashpoints come from. You can trace them back to certain events in your past, including both the good— and the bad—experiences you've had with various people, places, situations, and things. Many of these experiences you remember well, some less well, and some not at all; that is, until some person, place, thing, or situation reminds you.
- On the other hand, some of your flashpoints and fireworks may appear to have no connection with anything you can put your finger on, past or present. It could also be something so deeply buried that you don't (and maybe never will) know how it got there.

- Sometimes, you just can't explain _why_ something is a flashpoint or a firework for you, any more than you can explain why you find someone charismatic or sexy, or why you think panda bears are cute, or why some music makes you want to get up and dance and some music makes you want to get up and leave.
- Similarly, it's often impossible to explain why something _isn't_ a flashpoint or a firework for you... It just isn't.

3.6 RELATIONSHIP FLASHPOINTS AND FIREWORKS

To gain a better understanding of the feelings that arise in conflict, let's now turn to relationship flashpoints and fireworks. Relationship flashpoints are the things that people do that, in everyday language, "drive you around the bend," "get under your skin" or "get your goat." Relationship flashpoints can leave you feeling angry, disappointed, hurt, offended, resentful and so forth.

There are dozens of relationship flashpoints. Some of the most common ones include:

- unfairness/inequity
- being bossed around
- someone trying to cram some idea or belief down your throat
- being publicly shamed or humiliated
- being taken advantage of
- being talked down to
- being told that you "measure up"
- cheating of any kind
- criticism
- disrespect
- having your dignity taken away
- ridicule
- rejection

- someone violating your personal space (i.e., getting too close to you or "in your face").

We've all got relationship flashpoints so it's inevitable that sooner or later someone triggers one of yours. ***Because relationship flashpoints can cost you so much emotionally, they are the major source of psychological loss in conflict.*** The more often you experience flashpoints with someone, the greater the emotional, or psychological, cost is to you of that relationship.

Of course, we all have relationship fireworks too (without which, who would want to be in any kind of relationship with anyone?). ***You can think of relationship fireworks as the emotional glue that holds relationships together.*** Some common relationship fireworks include being loved or liked, accepted, acknowledged, praised, thanked, shown affection or appreciation, respected, looked up to, and admired.

In close relationships your fireworks are the sorts of things that you both love to do together and that spark moments in which you feel the most connected and alive. These are the moments that can make time stand still for both of you, and in which you can "lose" yourselves in fun, laughter, excitement, peace, happiness, pleasure, joy, delight, and contentment.

**Re-establishing the fireworks of a damaged relationship
can go a long way to repairing it.**

The Gift of Relationship Flashpoint and Fireworks Awareness

Flashpoints and fireworks exist on both sides of any relationship; and all relationships develop their own unique menu of fireworks (the specifics of which depend on the people in the relationship, and the nature of their relationship). All relationships also develop their own unique list of flashpoints to try to avoid. *So, in any kind of relationship self-awareness and communication are key to arriving at a mutual awareness of the relationship fireworks and flashpoints you have in common.*

Awareness can lead to many great things in any kind of relationship. Can awareness avert conflict? Yes! Simply knowing the other person's flashpoints as well as knowing your own is a great first step in both conflict prevention and conflict resolution. Furthermore, with this awareness, it gets faster and easier to recognize and appreciate what is going on when you are triggered by a flashpoint, as well as recognize what is going on with the other person when they are triggered too.

Understanding **why** something has become a relationship flashpoint for you or the other person is often good, but not always necessary. Quite often, just knowing what they are is all either of you need to know.

3.7 PUTTING YOUR RELATIONSHIP FIREWORKS AND FLASHPOINTS INTO WORDS

"The beginning of wisdom is calling things by their right name."
CONFUCIUS (CHINESE PHILOSOPHER, 551 B.C.–479 B.C.)

As I said in Chapter 2, the best starting point in conflict resolution is clarity. But to resolve conflicts, you need to be able to communicate what it is you're clear in your mind about. One of the most important things to be clear about and to make clear to the other person is how you are feeling and why. This exercise helps set the stage for that to happen.

- It's critical to communicate how you feel and what specifically it is that the other person does to evoke these feelings. For a lot of people, you must tell them, otherwise they won't know!
- This is true of both fireworks feelings and flashpoint feelings. And, by the way, when it comes to communicating fireworks feelings, telling someone what it is they do that makes you feel good can be a firework for them—and one that can also set off a few more between the two of you.
- There's no guarantee that telling the other person what flashpoints they are triggering in you, and how this makes you feel will change their behavior—but not saying anything will almost certainly guarantee that nothing changes.
- Don't worry about how eloquently you put whatever it is you want to say. You don't need to be a poet. What's far more important is *that* you say it! Saying something that doesn't come out quite right—whether it's about flashpoints or fireworks—can be better than saying nothing at all.
- When you say something important to the other person—especially if it's something you've wanted to say for a long time—it is then "out there" between the two of you, and it usually cannot be "taken back." And what is more, sometimes, whatever elephant there may have been in the room will no longer have anywhere to hide...

- To be sure, many things are easier said than done, but whatever it is that the two of you need to do to resolve your conflict, something must usually be said first!
- If you want to try this exercise together with someone, it's a good idea to start with the fireworks you have with each other, before moving on to your flashpoints. Sometimes, timing is everything.

> *"The time to repair the roof is when the sun is shining."*
>
> JOHN F. KENNEDY
> (35TH PRESIDENT OF THE UNITED STATES, 1917–1963)

Note that when putting either your relationship fireworks or your relationship flashpoints into words, consider how close you are to one another before telling them. This goes for fireworks and flashpoints, but it is especially important when it comes to telling the other person about the things they do that are flashpoints for you.

If you're not sure, do these exercises for your own benefit, and share what you're comfortable sharing with the other person when you feel the time is right.

3.7.1 PUTTING YOUR RELATIONSHIP FIREWORKS INTO WORDS

Some of the words in the lists for both fireworks and flashpoints
have similar meanings, and some have more than one meaning. This
means that different people can interpret some words differently.
This is unavoidable. So, interpret the words in these lists in your own
way and choose the ones that would come naturally to you if you
were to use them when talking to the other person.

Worksheets for this exercise are available from
www.theconflictresolvingnetwork.com

Note that you can either think of the relationship fireworks you
have with a particular person, or of your relationship fireworks in
general, but this exercise is more helpful when you do it with someone in mind. First, read over the list of fireworks character traits.
Think of the character traits that mean the most to you that the
person you're thinking of shows. Add any that are not on the list.
Next, read the list of fireworks feelings.

Third, connect the fireworks traits the other person shows and
the fireworks feelings that you feel when they show those traits. It's
helpful if you can think of certain specific situations or specific
instances. It can also be especially helpful if these are ones that
both of you are likely to remember in case you decide to share your
list or do this exercise together. After you're done, you could summarize your fireworks like this:

My Fireworks with Andrew

When Andrew and I:

- ✓ binge-watch some show that we're both crazy about
- ✓ do DIY stuff together
- ✓ share a chuckle over one of our "inside" jokes
- ✓ fall asleep in each other's arms

When Andrew:

- ✓ goes out of his way to be nice to my mom who can be kind of difficult
- ✓ becomes a kid again when he plays with the kids

These are the things I feel: Cherished, attractive, light, carefree and safe.

Any specific instances come to mind? Lots. Too many to think of off the top of my head.

The positivity account "balance" you have with someone is built mainly on the fireworks moments you share.

My Fireworks Character List with _____ .

It is a big firework for me when _____ shows how _____ he/she/they are (or can be).

- ❑ Adventurous
- ❑ Affectionate
- ❑ Agreeable
- ❑ Altruistic
- ❑ Ambitious
- ❑ Articulate

❑ Artistic
❑ Assertive
❑ Attractive
❑ Authentic
❑ Balanced
❑ Calm
❑ Careful
❑ Caring
❑ Charismatic
❑ Charming
❑ Cheerful
❑ Clear
❑ Compassionate
❑ Competitive
❑ Confident
❑ Conscientious
❑ Conservative
❑ Considerate
❑ Cool
❑ Courageous
❑ Courteous
❑ Creative
❑ Decisive
❑ Deep
❑ Dependable
❑ Determined
❑ Devoted
❑ Devout
❑ Down-to-earth
❑ Driven
❑ Easygoing
❑ Emotional
❑ Enthusiastic
❑ Expressive

❑ Extroverted
❑ Fair
❑ Feisty
❑ Friendly
❑ Full of energy
❑ Fun-loving
❑ Funny
❑ Generous
❑ Gentle
❑ Handy
❑ Happy
❑ Happy-go-lucky
❑ Honest
❑ Humble
❑ Imaginative
❑ Independent
❑ Influential
❑ Informed
❑ Insightful
❑ Inspiring
❑ Intelligent
❑ Introverted
❑ Intuitive
❑ Involved
❑ Kind
❑ Knowledgeable
❑ Liberal
❑ Likable
❑ Logical
❑ Loving
❑ Loyal
❑ Mature
❑ Modest
❑ Nurturing

- ❑ Open
- ❑ Optimistic
- ❑ Organized
- ❑ Outdoorsy
- ❑ Outgoing
- ❑ Outspoken
- ❑ Passionate
- ❑ Patient
- ❑ Perceptive
- ❑ Philosophical
- ❑ Playful
- ❑ Polite
- ❑ Positive
- ❑ Powerful
- ❑ Practical
- ❑ Precise
- ❑ Professional
- ❑ Proper
- ❑ Protective
- ❑ Proud
- ❑ Punctual
- ❑ Questioning
- ❑ Quick
- ❑ Quirky
- ❑ Rational
- ❑ Rebellious
- ❑ Refined
- ❑ Relaxed
- ❑ Reliable
- ❑ Religious
- ❑ Respected
- ❑ Respectful
- ❑ Romantic
- ❑ Rugged

- ❑ Secure
- ❑ Self-aware
- ❑ Sense of humor
- ❑ Sensitive
- ❑ Sexy
- ❑ Shy
- ❑ Sincere
- ❑ Soft-spoken
- ❑ Spiritual
- ❑ Sporty
- ❑ Stable
- ❑ Strong
- ❑ Sweet
- ❑ Talented
- ❑ Tenacious
- ❑ Thoughtful
- ❑ Tidy
- ❑ Tolerant
- ❑ Tough
- ❑ Tough-minded
- ❑ Trusting
- ❑ Trustworthy
- ❑ Unconventional
- ❑ Understanding
- ❑ Unique
- ❑ Unpretentious
- ❑ Unselfish
- ❑ Vulnerable
- ❑ Warm
- ❑ Well mannered
- ❑ Witty
- ❑ Young at heart

Any other fireworks character traits?

My Fireworks List of Fireworks Feelings with _____ .

When _____ (shows character traits and/or does specific things that are a firework for me), **I feel:** _____ .

- ❑ Accepted
- ❑ Admiration
- ❑ Admired
- ❑ Adored
- ❑ Affection
- ❑ Amazement
- ❑ Appreciated
- ❑ Appreciation
- ❑ At one with you
- ❑ At peace
- ❑ Attraction
- ❑ Attractive
- ❑ Awe
- ❑ Belonging
- ❑ Blessed
- ❑ Bliss
- ❑ Bonding
- ❑ Calm
- ❑ Cherished
- ❑ Close
- ❑ Comfort

- ❑ Confident
- ❑ Contented
- ❑ Courage
- ❑ Delight
- ❑ Desire (e.g., desire for you and desired by you)
- ❑ Devotion
- ❑ Ecstatic
- ❑ Elated
- ❑ Empathy
- ❑ Encouraged
- ❑ Energized
- ❑ Enthusiastic
- ❑ Euphoric
- ❑ Excited
- ❑ Faith (e.g., faith in myself, you, us)
- ❑ Fascination
- ❑ Fondness
- ❑ Forgiven
- ❑ Forgiveness

- ❏ Fulfilled
- ❏ Grateful
- ❏ Happy
- ❏ Honored
- ❏ Hopeful
- ❏ Inspired
- ❏ Joyful
- ❏ Light and carefree
- ❏ Like "a million bucks"
- ❏ Liking
- ❏ Love (e.g., love toward you, loved by you)
- ❏ Optimistic
- ❏ Passion
- ❏ Playful
- ❏ Pleasure
- ❏ Pride (e.g., proud of me, proud of you)

- ❏ Relaxed
- ❏ Respect (e.g., respect for myself, respect for you)
- ❏ Respected
- ❏ Romantic
- ❏ Safe
- ❏ Secure
- ❏ Self-confident
- ❏ Serene
- ❏ Special
- ❏ Strong
- ❏ Thrilled
- ❏ Trust
- ❏ Uplifted
- ❏ Warmth
- ❏ Welcomed
- ❏ Worthy

Any other fireworks feelings and specific instances?

Interested in extending this exercise further?

Consider doing this exercise again, but this time from the point of view of the other person. In other words, ask yourself "What are the things about me, and the things I do that are fireworks for _____?"

3.7.2 PUTTING YOUR RELATIONSHIP FLASHPOINTS INTO WORDS

For this exercise, I've drawn up three lists: Common flashpoint character traits, common flashpoint feelings, and a list of specific things that people do that are often relationship flashpoints. As with the fireworks exercise, you can either think of a particular person, or relationship flashpoints in general, but this exercise is more helpful when you do it with someone in mind—ideally, the same person who you had in mind when you completed your fireworks list.

> ⬇ **Worksheets for this exercise are available from**
> **www.theconflictresolvingnetwork.com**

- First, read over the list of flashpoint character traits. What are the traits that trigger you the most, when the person you're thinking of shows them? Lots of people are bugged at least a little bit by most of the flashpoints on this list—so check off only those that are ***really big*** ones for you. Add any that are not the list.
- As with your fireworks, it is good to think of certain situations or specific instances (and note how often they happen). So, in addition to the flashpoint traits list, read through the list of specific relationship flashpoints. It is especially helpful if the instances you remember are ones the other person is likely to remember too, in case you decide to share your list, or if you do this exercise together. Add any for yourself that are not on that list as well.
- The idea is to connect which traits or specific things the other person does with the flashpoint feelings that you feel when this happens. So, once you've got the list of your flashpoint traits and specifics, go to the list of

flashpoint feelings. For each one, note all the feelings each of the flashpoints you identified trigger in you. After you're done, you can summarize your flashpoints like this:

Example: My Flashpoints with Andrew

When Andrew:

- ✓ doesn't listen
- ✓ criticizes things I value and respect
- ✓ puts down people I respect and admire
- ✓ says "Whatever!"

These are the things I feel: Angry, exasperated, humiliated, and hurt.

How often do these things happen? Often enough to make it a real problem!

Any specific instances come to mind?

The other night when we went to this party, Andrew started talking about politics again even though I told him he shouldn't do that with some of my friends. He got into a heated debate with Brittany over something about the environment and said things that put her down—or at least put her ideas down. He made me—and her—extremely uncomfortable by what he said. I was so embarrassed! He can be very opinionated and rude, especially when he gets going on something he believes in strongly.

My Flashpoints with _____ .

Character traits that he/she/they sometimes show that are flashpoints for me.

- ❏ Aggressiveness
- ❏ Aloofness
- ❏ Anger
- ❏ Anxiousness
- ❏ Apathy
- ❏ Argumentativeness
- ❏ Arrogance
- ❏ Bigotry
- ❏ Being a fake
- ❏ Being closed and uncommunicative
- ❏ Being unemotional
- ❏ Being unromantic
- ❏ Bossiness
- ❏ Bullying
- ❏ Callousness
- ❏ Capriciousness
- ❏ Carelessness
- ❏ Chauvinism
- ❏ Childishness
- ❏ Clinginess
- ❏ Coldness
- ❏ Conceit
- ❏ Condescension
- ❏ Cowardliness
- ❏ Criticism
- ❏ Defensiveness
- ❏ Desperation
- ❏ Dishonesty
- ❏ Disinterest
- ❏ Discouraging
- ❏ Disorganization
- ❏ Disrespect
- ❏ Distancing
- ❏ Foolishness
- ❏ Greed
- ❏ Gullibility
- ❏ Hardheartedness
- ❏ Helplessness
- ❏ Hostility
- ❏ Hypocrisy
- ❏ Ignorance
- ❏ Immaturity
- ❏ Impatience
- ❏ Indecisiveness
- ❏ Insecurity
- ❏ Insincerity
- ❏ Instability
- ❏ Intimidation
- ❏ Jealousy
- ❏ Judgmental
- ❏ Lateness
- ❏ Laziness
- ❏ Loudness
- ❏ Meanness
- ❏ Messiness
- ❏ Moodiness
- ❏ Mood swings
- ❏ Neediness
- ❏ Negativity
- ❏ Neuroticism
- ❏ Overly emotional
- ❏ Overly rational
- ❏ Pessimism
- ❏ Pettiness
- ❏ Possessiveness
- ❏ Preachiness
- ❏ Pushiness

- ☐ Ridicule
- ☐ Rigidity (e.g., with rules)
- ☐ Rudeness
- ☐ Sarcasm
- ☐ Secretiveness
- ☐ Self-centeredness
- ☐ Self-doubting
- ☐ Selfishness
- ☐ Self-pity
- ☐ Self-righteousness
- ☐ Sexism
- ☐ Sloppiness
- ☐ Smugness

- ☐ Snobbery
- ☐ Spitefulness
- ☐ Stinginess
- ☐ Stubbornness
- ☐ Suspiciousness
- ☐ Thoughtlessness
- ☐ Unassertiveness
- ☐ Unavailability
- ☐ Unfairness
- ☐ Unpredictability
- ☐ Vulgarity
- ☐ Wastefulness

Any other flashpoint character traits?

My Flashpoints with _____ .

Specific things that he/she/they sometimes does that are flashpoints for me.

- ☐ Accuses me of things I would never do
- ☐ Acts "holier-than-thou"
- ☐ Acts as if they are entitled to things they are not entitled to
- ☐ Acts carelessly
- ☐ Acts like a know-it-all
- ☐ Acts like they're better than everyone else
- ☐ Assumes I don't know what I'm talking about

- ❑ Assumes I'm lying
- ❑ Assumes the worst about me
- ❑ Backs me into a corner so I feel like I have no choice
- ❑ Baits me or tries to start a fight
- ❑ Borrows or takes stuff of mine without asking
- ❑ Bosses me around
- ❑ Brags
- ❑ Breaks a promise
- ❑ Bullies me
- ❑ Calls me names
- ❑ Calls me stupid
- ❑ Cheats at something
- ❑ Checks up on me
- ❑ Cries
- ❑ Criticizes me
- ❑ Criticizes or puts me down for having the flashpoints that I have
- ❑ Demands that I provide proof of what I said I did or didn't do
- ❑ Does things behind my back
- ❑ Doesn't admit to any fault
- ❑ Doesn't apologize
- ❑ Doesn't ask me for my help
- ❑ Doesn't believe me
- ❑ Doesn't do their fair share of the work
- ❑ Doesn't know—or forgets—important facts or details
- ❑ Doesn't let me get a word in edgewise
- ❑ Doesn't listen
- ❑ Doesn't reciprocate when I do little things to show how much I care
- ❑ Doesn't stick up for me
- ❑ Doesn't stick up for themselves
- ❑ Doesn't thank me
- ❑ Doubts or questions my judgement
- ❑ Dredges up negative things in the past and dwells on them
- ❑ Embarrasses me

- ❑ Feels sorry for themselves
- ❑ Fishes for compliments
- ❑ Flirts
- ❑ Focuses on the negative
- ❑ Forbids me to do things
- ❑ Forgets important dates—birthdays, etc.
- ❑ Gaslights me
- ❑ Gets drunk or high
- ❑ Ghosts me then after a while comes back
- ❑ Gives me advice even if I say I don't want it
- ❑ Gives me advice without asking if I want it
- ❑ Gives me the silent treatment
- ❑ Glares at me
- ❑ Gossips
- ❑ Hangs up on me
- ❑ Has to have the last word
- ❑ Hides things from me
- ❑ Hogs the limelight
- ❑ Holds a grudge
- ❑ Ignores me
- ❑ Interrogates me
- ❑ Is a "bleeding heart"
- ❑ Is demanding
- ❑ Is late for important things
- ❑ Jokes in a mean-spirited way
- ❑ Keeps interrupting me
- ❑ Lacks confidence
- ❑ Lacks confidence in me
- ❑ Lashes out
- ❑ Laughs at me
- ❑ Lies to me
- ❑ Loafs around and does nothing
- ❑ Looks weak
- ❑ Loses patience

- ❏ Makes comments that are racist, sexist, etc.
- ❏ Makes snide remarks
- ❏ Micromanages me
- ❏ Minimizes the impact my flashpoints have on me
- ❏ Minimizes the importance of what I think and how I feel
- ❏ Mocks me
- ❏ Mutters things under their breath
- ❏ Nags me about _____ .
- ❏ Nitpicks
- ❏ Picks on me or others
- ❏ Plays "the victim"
- ❏ Points their finger at me
- ❏ Pouts
- ❏ Pretends to be an expert
- ❏ Pushes me
- ❏ Puts down, or makes fun of, my fireworks or flashpoints (e.g., says they're childish, stupid, weird, etc.)
- ❏ Puts down my friends
- ❏ Puts down my ideas
- ❏ Puts down my values
- ❏ Puts down or minimizes my accomplishments
- ❏ Puts down people I respect and admire
- ❏ Puts me down
- ❏ Puts me on the spot
- ❏ Puts words in my mouth
- ❏ Raises their voice at me
- ❏ Rebuffs/rejects me
- ❏ Refuses my help
- ❏ Refuses to answer my questions
- ❏ Reneges on promises
- ❏ Rolls their eyes
- ❏ Says "Take it easy, don't get so wound up!", etc.
- ❏ Says "I told you so."
- ❏ Says "What's wrong with you?" or "What's the matter with you?"

- ❑ Says "Whatever!"
- ❑ Says "Who cares?"
- ❑ Says one thing, does another
- ❑ Says or does something stupid
- ❑ Says something nice then, right after, something mean
- ❑ Sends double messages (e.g., gives backhanded compliments)
- ❑ Shames me (when we're alone or in front of others)
- ❑ Shoots down my ideas
- ❑ Shuts me down
- ❑ Slams the door
- ❑ Smirks
- ❑ Snitches
- ❑ Snubs me
- ❑ Spies on me
- ❑ Spreads rumors
- ❑ Stonewalls
- ❑ Stubbornly sticks to rules
- ❑ Sulks
- ❑ Swears
- ❑ Takes me for granted
- ❑ Takes over (e.g., discussions)
- ❑ Takes undue credit
- ❑ Talks behind my back
- ❑ Talks down to me
- ❑ Taunts me
- ❑ Teases me in a mean way
- ❑ Tells me (or implies) that I don't "measure up"
- ❑ Tells me what I'm thinking or feeling
- ❑ Tells me what I'm supposed to be thinking, feeling, or doing
- ❑ Tells off-color jokes
- ❑ Treats me (or others) unfairly
- ❑ Tries to cram some idea or belief down my throat
- ❑ Tries to make me feel guilty to get me to do something
- ❑ Tries to take advantage of me

- ❏ Trivializes my accomplishments
- ❏ Trivializes my feelings
- ❏ Twists things I say
- ❏ Questions or doubts my authority
- ❏ Questions or doubts my knowledge or ability
- ❏ Undermines my authority
- ❏ Upstages me
- ❏ Uses things I've confided in about myself against me
- ❏ Violates my personal space (e.g., sits or stands too close to me)
- ❏ Wags their finger at me
- ❏ Won't take "I don't agree with you." for an answer
- ❏ Yells at me

Any other specific things that _____ does that are flashpoints for you?

My Flashpoint Feelings

When _____ (shows certain traits and/or does specific things that are a flashpoint for me), **I feel:**

- ❏ Abandoned
- ❏ Agitated
- ❏ Ambivalent
- ❏ Angry
- ❏ Anguished
- ❏ Annoyed
- ❏ Anxious

- ❏ Apathetic
- ❏ Apprehensive
- ❏ Ashamed
- ❏ Awkward
- ❏ Betrayed
- ❏ Bewildered
- ❏ Bitter

- ☐ Bored
- ☐ Confused
- ☐ Contempt
- ☐ Defeated
- ☐ Depleted
- ☐ Despair
- ☐ Desperate
- ☐ Disappointed
- ☐ Disapproved of
- ☐ Discouraged
- ☐ Disgusted
- ☐ Disrespected
- ☐ Distrustful
- ☐ Drained
- ☐ Dread
- ☐ Embarrassed
- ☐ Enraged
- ☐ Exasperated
- ☐ Exhausted/fatigued
- ☐ Fearful
- ☐ Fed up
- ☐ Frustrated
- ☐ Grief
- ☐ Guilty
- ☐ Hate
- ☐ Heartbroken
- ☐ Helpless
- ☐ Hopeless
- ☐ Humiliated
- ☐ Hurt
- ☐ Inadequate
- ☐ Infuriated
- ☐ Insecure
- ☐ Insulted

- ☐ Irritated
- ☐ Jealous
- ☐ Left out
- ☐ Let down
- ☐ Like a fool
- ☐ Like I'm being forced against my will, and it gets my back up
- ☐ Loathing
- ☐ Lonely
- ☐ Neglected
- ☐ Offended
- ☐ On thin ice
- ☐ Outraged
- ☐ Panicky
- ☐ Pity
- ☐ Rage
- ☐ Regret
- ☐ Rejected
- ☐ Remorse
- ☐ Resentment
- ☐ Resigned
- ☐ Sad
- ☐ Shocked
- ☐ Sickened
- ☐ Snubbed
- ☐ Spiteful
- ☐ Stressed
- ☐ Stupid
- ☐ Suspicious
- ☐ Terrified
- ☐ Trapped
- ☐ Uncertain
- ☐ Undignified

❏ Unheard   ❏ Weak
❏ Unsafe   ❏ Weird
❏ Unworthy   ❏ Worried
❏ Wary

Any other flashpoint feelings?

Interested in extending this exercise further?

As with your fireworks, consider doing this exercise again,
but this time from the point of view of the other person. Ask yourself:
"What are the things about me, and what are the things I sometimes
do that are–or could be–flashpoints for _____?"

4

CONFLICT-PRONE RELATIONSHIPS

What's Coming Up in this Chapter...

Even the closest, strongest, and happiest of relationships experience occasional turbulence. However, certain kinds of relationships are particularly prone to conflict, which means that being in any one of them can not only intensify any conflict that's already going on but can also easily set off new ones.

In Chapter 2, I introduced the term foundational conflict. As I said, foundational conflict tends to be deeply entrenched and has a long history of unresolved disagreements, fights and so forth, together with grudges on both sides. Foundationally conflicted relationships contain fundamental incompatibilities between the two people involved so that, typically, these relationships cycle from quarrel or fight to some degree of resolution, then sooner or later, back again to yet another quarrel or fight, over and over again, indefinitely.

In addition to foundationally conflicted relationships, there are eight more conflict-prone relationships to be mindful of: Strained, draining, ambivalent, stretched, square-peg-round-hole, lop-sided, lop-sided three-way and uncharted territory relationships. The purpose of this chapter is to introduce you to all eight of them.

4.1 STRAINED RELATIONSHIPS

In a strained relationship, the minuses exceed the plusses, and as much as both of you would like to, neither of you can pull out of it, or at least not easily. In a nutshell, strained relationships are those you can't easily get out of (or at all), with people you're not particularly fond of, and who usually aren't particularly fond of you. I'm sure you can think of one or two relationships in your life that fit, or have fitted, this description.

Surefire signs of relationship strain include feeling your teeth clench and stomach tighten into a knot every time the other person's around, and all the while feeling like you're walking on eggshells or sitting on a powder keg waiting for the next "blow up" which you know could happen any time.

A strained relationship is among the most conflict-prone for at least two reasons. First, anger at one another and resentment (as well as often other emotions such as hurt, distrust or contempt) are never far from the surface, so it doesn't take much to set off yet another conflict. The second reason is that, if the conflict has been going on for years, both parties know each other's most potent flashpoints well... and know how to use them.

The conflict in strained relationships is like the conflict in foundationally conflicted relationships. As with all foundational conflicts, strained relationships can cycle from conflict to some degree of resolution and then right back again–sooner or later–to another conflict. However, the difference is that it's easier to repair a strained relationship.

4.2 DRAINING RELATIONSHIPS

Although there are many different ways that relationships can be draining, the relationships I'm thinking of here are the ones you have with people who, for whatever reason, rub you the wrong way, but to whom you must be kind, friendly, polite, or just plain civil. What makes this sort of relationship draining is the amount of willpower it takes on your part to be kind, friendly, polite, or just plain civil. Restraining yourself, biting your tongue, forcing smiles, and pretending to agree about things you disagree on just to keep the peace, all takes self-control which takes effort, and effort takes willpower.

Now the thing is, your willpower is limited. You only have so much willpower to draw upon on a given day, and as the day goes on you spend it. You spend it doing all the things you need to do that take willpower; and, if it's been a particularly long day, you're "tapped out" and can barely lift a finger. So, depending on how many other things you've got on your plate that demand a lot of willpower (e.g., kids, a long commute, being on a tight budget or a diet, or having a never-ending "To Do" list), draining relationships can be particularly... well, draining.

This is especially the case when these relationships are with people you must deal with all day, every day. But even if your contact is occasional, you can come away completely exhausted after being around one of these people for just an hour at a work, or a social function.

Draining relationships are conflict-prone for a couple of reasons: First, psychological loss tends to be magnified when you're feeling depleted to begin with, so it's easy to go from annoyed to exasperated in an instant. The second reason is that draining relationships typically cost you more than you'd like them to cost and have many minuses to them. This means that when that person does something that creates a loss for you, you don't have much in your "positivity account" with them to draw upon, so you'll likely be putting that loss on your emotional credit card.

Like strained relationships, draining relationships can carry
around a lot of unresolved conflict and can become foundational
in nature. Tensions and differences are never far from the
surface in these relationships. Conflicts in strained or draining
relationships, when they do erupt, tend to be especially heated
and can suddenly and unexpectedly bring out the worst in us.

4.3 AMBIVALENT RELATIONSHIPS

What is Ambivalence?

Many people think ambivalence means the same thing as ambigu-
ity, apathy, or indifference; well, it's anything but! Ambivalence
means having mixed, contradictory and conflicting feelings about
someone or something. We all have mixed feelings about lots of
people, places and things (e.g., celebrities, restaurants we've been to,
or modern art). Ordinarily, ambivalence isn't particularly bothersome so long as whoever or whatever it is you have conflicting
feelings about doesn't really matter all that much to you.

Ambivalence isn't particularly bothersome either, even when
you have mixed feelings about someone who does matter, so long
as, overall, you're OK with the relationship and the plusses clearly
outweigh the minuses. In these situations, you tend to shrug off,
accept whatever it is about the relationship that you have mixed
feelings about, and take it all in stride (e.g., "I love my job, though
I'm not crazy about the hours."; "I love my teenage son, but like most
kids his age, he never listens to a word I say."; or, "I may not agree
with everything my brother-in-law says, but fundamentally, he's an
OK guy."). *However, it's a completely different matter when you
have conflicting feelings about someone who matters to you and*

the question of whether the minuses outweigh the plusses hangs in the balance.

Ambivalence also arises when you have to make an important decision in your life that involves people who matter to you, and when you have to choose between two conflicting courses of action: Leave a relationship or stay? Marry or stay single? Accept a proposal of marriage or not? Leave a marriage or not? Have children or not? Accept Job Offer A or Job Offer B? Stay in your job or start looking for a new one? Stay in your job or just plain quit? Switch careers? Move to another city? Move to another country?

What can make these decisions especially difficult and for ambivalence to be set off is when:

- first, not making a decision is not an option (i.e., sooner or later you'll have to decide);
- second, the two options are mutually exclusive (i.e., choosing one means saying no to the other); and,
- third, both courses of action look good in their own way.

For example, Job Offer A looks good and Job Offer B looks good too. Both jobs have their plusses and minuses, but they each have different plusses and minuses. For example, Job A has higher pay but B is closer to home; Job A has more opportunity for advancement, but B is more secure; and, Job A has more potential for professional growth but B has more prestige. So, choosing Job A means saying goodbye to some plusses that matter to you, and choosing Job B means saying goodbye to other plusses... plusses that also matter to you... but for different reasons.

Ambivalence then involves going back and forth (sometimes over a long time—even years) between thoughts and feelings in favor of one option and thoughts and feelings in favor of the other. It's because there are both plusses and minuses to both options that you can really feel torn. Why torn? Because, for example, in a romantic relationship some part of you (let's say your "practical side") wants what comes with one choice but not the other, and another part of you (let's call it your "romantic side") wants exactly the opposite.

> *"In any moment of decision, the best thing you can do is the right thing, the next best thing is the wrong thing, and the worst thing you can do is nothing."*
>
> THEODORE ROOSEVELT (1858–1919)

One thing that many people do (and perhaps you've tried this), is to draw up a list of "pros" and "cons." It could be the pros and cons of staying in a relationship, the pros and cons of leaving a relationship, or the pros and cons of a career choice, and so on.

Always remember this: One pro can outweigh a dozen cons, and one con can outweigh a dozen pros. For that matter, one pro can outweigh all the cons put together. And, of course, all the pros you can think of can, sometimes, be outweighed by a single con.

The Ambivalent Relationship

Relationship ambivalence often begins with the other person (let's say it's someone with whom you have an important—or at least promising—relationship) doing something that results in a sudden discrepancy between what you'd hoped or expected to see and what you're seeing. When this happens, what you are likely to feel is a queasy, uncomfortable tension arising from the fact that although there are many positives to this person and your relationship, something's definitely "not quite right."

If not clarified or resolved (e.g., "What did you mean when you said....? or Why did you...?") or fixed outright, and if you continue to see more of the same discrepancy as time goes on, then it won't take long for conflicting feelings—and ambivalence—to take hold.

Once ambivalence takes hold, you begin going back and forth between negative and positive thoughts and feelings about the person and your relationship with them:

- "This is not what I signed up for... Wait a minute, let's not jump the gun..."
- "This isn't going to work.... No, everything's going to work out fine."
- "I don't think this is what I want... Hang on, let's give things a little more time and see what develops...".

The Ambivalent Relationship Rollercoaster

It's this back and forth between being positively and then negatively inclined that makes ambivalence an emotional rollercoaster ride: Sometimes, you want to say yes, but then you want to say no; sometimes you want to stay, but then you want to go; sometimes you want to stay away, but then you want to come back; sometimes you want to say something, but then you don't; sometimes you want to click the "block" button, but then you don't... (I think you get the picture).

Typically, things get even worse if nothing gets clarified, resolved or fixed, and the discrepancy is as obvious as ever. This is because despite the plusses to your relationship, sooner or later you reach a fork in the road at which point you realize that you must finally do something. Ambivalence now kicks into high gear as you realize you've reached an impasse for which there is no easy answer, and from which there is no easy way out. Earlier on, your decision might have been either to say something (and risk hurting the other person's feelings) or not say anything (and hope for the best); now, however, it may well have come to a far more difficult decision such as stay vs. leave the relationship altogether.

Until the impasse between the positives and the negatives is resolved and you can finally decide one way or the other, relationship ambivalence can feel like an "all consuming" tug-of-war, which can drain you to the point of exhaustion.

Relationship Ambivalence and Conflict

Ambivalence is a form of inner conflict; and when you've got inner conflict, outer conflict isn't far behind.

If you are—or have ever been—ambivalent about someone, or are or have been in any sort of relationship with someone who was ambivalent about you, you'll recognize these telltale signs of relationship ambivalence. When ambivalent about someone, people typically:

- Run warm and cold. When feeling positive about their relationship (i.e., on the "upswing" of the rollercoaster ride), they're warm. When they start changing their mind again, they're cold.
- They drag their heels on making any further signs of deepening commitment until they make up their mind; in other words, they try to stall or "buy time" while they're trying to decide, all of which to you looks like they're procrastinating or just don't care.
- They sometimes seem preoccupied, easily distracted, disengaged, distant or even dismissive; and when asked about it, are usually reluctant to say why and quickly try and change the subject.

- People in relationship ambivalence tend to be less than forthright about how they're really feeling because it's hard to be totally open and honest with someone you're ambivalent about. This doesn't mean that ambivalent people become out and out liars—it's just that they don't share as many thoughts and feelings with you as they could.

Communication is one of the first casualties of ambivalence in any relationship.

- Ambivalent people are often overly sensitive to and watchful for anything about you that bothers them even in the slightest—often becoming short-tempered, nitpicky, touchy, and harping on even the littlest things—things that had never mattered much before.
- In relationship ambivalence, people often mentally withdraw from the relationship, and, if their ambivalence has grown strong enough, begin to simply "go along" with whatever their role is in their relationship until they decide what to do.
- If relationship ambivalence gets intense enough, people may start dropping hints about their discontent with the other person in passive aggressive ways. As you may recall from Chapter 3, passive aggression can also include doing things like openly commenting and complaining about someone's shortcomings to other people, withholding what someone wants (and making up some lie to rationalize or try to excuse it), making snide remarks that are explained away as "just kidding," teasing that's mean spirited rather than friendly and light-hearted, making sarcastic comments that cut a little too close to the bone, and muttering comments under their breath, or making thinly veiled jokes at your expense.

- Finally, when ambivalent people feel more positive about their relationship (i.e., are warm), they sometimes "overdo" it by making overly positive statements or promises, which they then renege or otherwise backpedal on.

**In ambivalence, plans and promises often fade
as quickly as they are made.**

Given all the preceding, it's understandable that ambivalence is present in almost every conflict. There are many reasons why ambivalent relationships are conflict-prone:

- Not only is ambivalence hard on the person who's ambivalent, it's also hard on the recipient of it. Being on the receiving end of ambivalence becomes an emotional rollercoaster ride too; for example, when moments of warmth, closeness and attunement are felt one day, only to be followed by coldness, indifference, and aloofness the next.
- ***Ambivalence is the mother of all mixed (a.k.a. double) messages!*** Mixed messages create a great deal of confusion and frustration because:
  - The recipient is never sure which message to believe (e.g., is it the warm message or the cold message?).
  - Mixed messages can keep the other person on edge, guessing and hanging on.
  - People on the receiving end of ambivalence often end up being ecstatic and get their hopes up when they hear something they wanted to hear, or feel completely rejected, dejected, and frustrated when it's something they didn't want to hear.

○ People on the receiving end of ambivalence also tend to spend a lot of time and effort trying to figure out the meaning of whatever the other person did (or didn't do). This is often futile because ambivalent people's warm-then-cold behavior is hard to explain. Thoughts about what might be going on go around and around with no firm conclusion possible (i.e., rumination).

As mentioned in the previous chapter, rumination rarely leads to illumination, tending instead, to spawn inner escalation.

- Because ambivalence is so emotionally draining and toxic and uses up a great deal of mental energy, it adds dramatically to the psychological cost (i.e., the minuses) on _both_ sides of any relationship.
- Sometimes one or both people feel the temptation to pull the plug or even do something prematurely to "foreclose" on the relationship (e.g., sabotage the relationship), just to get out of the ambivalence or to get out of being on the receiving end of it.
- When ambivalent about someone, there can also be a temptation to have a "Plan B" or to "hold out" for someone "better" to come along, or actively look for someone "better" (e.g., on social media). The problem with this is that it weakens whatever commitment to the relationship they may have, as well as the motivation to work through whatever the impasse is together.
- At the same time, the other person can form their own "Plan B" which also lowers the investment they have in the ambivalent person. The stakes then don't seem as

high which, in turn, renders the ambivalent person's ups and downs less frustrating and hurtful.

- Ambivalence is often a factor in tempting one partner in a romantic relationship to cheat on the other. So, some people in ambivalence take advantage of social media to find past partners in the hopes of rekindling an old flame—or, for that matter, kindling a new one. Initially, this may be just to have someone "on standby" in case things don't work out, but it can easily go beyond that (note too that the person on the receiving end of an ambivalent relationship may be tempted to do exactly the same thing).

A Few Final Points about Relationship Ambivalence and Conflict

- Ambivalence can also arise at various decision points in the unfolding of a conflict (e.g., do I retaliate or not?). Worth noting as well is that ambivalence is commonly felt in the disengagement stage; if, for example, you're deciding whether or not to offer an olive branch.

The next chapter will help you to answer for yourself this most fundamental question in conflict resolution; that is, whether you want to resolve a conflict in the first place.

- Ambivalence in *you* can spark ambivalence in the *other person*, and when both of you become ambivalent about one another, the situation can get explosive!
- As distressing as ambivalence is for adults, it can be *extremely* distressing for children and adolescents (e.g., "I love my dad but I hate how he talks to my mom

sometimes."). Children and adolescents feel all the inner conflict that comes with ambivalence but can't put much of it into words, nor can they fully understand why they feel the way they do. Consequently, when ambivalent about someone, children and teens often become unusually moody, agitated, and touchy. Furthermore, they often act out their feelings with other people—friends, siblings, parents, teachers, etc.—who have nothing to do with whatever it is they're ambivalent about. Being ambivalent doesn't necessarily excuse their troubling behavior but it can help explain it.

4.4 STRETCHED RELATIONSHIPS

I define a stretched relationship as one that has gotten ahead of it-self. In other words, a stretched relationship is often one that has gone too far too fast. In a stretched relationship your attempts at forming closeness outstrip the fundamentals of where you are in your relationship and how well you know each other. Stretched relationships have a false sense of closeness that can be fun for a while, but the novelty can wear off quickly.

Getting into relationship stretch can come from over-socializing or getting too chummy with someone, or spending too much time with someone (i.e., too often and for too long, given how close you are) or revealing too much (such as private things) about yourself to someone too soon. Trying too hard to get on someone's "good side" can often cause relationship stretch. This is especially likely to happen when there's an ulterior motive behind being overly nice to someone (i.e., to get something from them). Even forcing people to get along who don't get along can put those relationships into some degree of stretch.

Stretch in romantic relationships can come from, for example, little things like using endearments (i.e., pet names) too soon, or bigger things like making commitments (or even discussing such plans) that neither of you are really ready or able to make yet, becoming intimate too soon, moving in together too soon, getting engaged too soon and marrying too soon. Sooner or later, particularly in a stretched romantic relationship, you find out something about the other person that you wished you'd known much sooner.

In addition to the desire for closeness, going too far too fast in any kind of relationship can be the result of wishful thinking that the rest of your relationship will somehow "catch up" to the stretch. Sure, there's a chance that it will; but if it doesn't, the problem is that sooner or later, something just won't feel right.

This happens when the assumptions you may have made—or illusions you may have had—about how "perfect" you are for one another begin to crumble. Other signs of relationship stretch are that for one or both of you, the relationship begins to feel hollow, and you begin to "go through the motions" when doing things that once meant a lot. Additional signs of relationship stretch are that one or both of you start feeling that you're on "thin ice" or out on a limb—making you over-sensitive and skittish about any signs of a real or perceived rift. This erodes trust and makes matters worse.

Trust is one of the first casualties of relationship stretch.

All this becomes a perfect set-up for conflict for three reasons. First, like being ambivalent about someone, you can't be in relationship stretch with someone for long; it's too emotionally draining—so, sooner or later, something will snap. The second thing that makes stretched relationships conflict-prone is that when one of you begins to pull back even a little bit, the other person is likely to feel snubbed or even scorned. The third reason is that in a stretched relationship, major blow ups can be quickly and easily triggered by even the slightest upset. Simply put, stretched relationships are prone to plummeting and, when they do, they plummet hard—indeed, the greater the stretch, the harder the fall! If the stretch comes from a genuine desire to be close (as it often does) then the fall in a stretched relationship can be particularly hard. If you've ever been in a stretched relationship, you may have been mystified at how quickly it fell apart after just one or two relatively minor (or so you thought) spats.

For couples in serious relationship stretch, their first "big fight" is often their last.

4.5 SQUARE-PEG-ROUND-HOLE RELATIONSHIPS

In Chapter 1, I mentioned that it is possible to experience psychological loss when you wish someone treated you a certain way, but they don't. This often feels like a loss even though, strictly speaking, it isn't really a loss if nothing was ever promised to you. Not getting what you want is not the same thing as losing what you already have. But the fact is that unfulfilled wants and expectations, even if unfounded, often feel like a loss. It is exactly this kind of loss people in square-peg-round-hole relationships feel all the time.

As everyone knows, you can't fit a square peg in a round hole. Of course, there's nothing wrong with square pegs or round holes per se, it's just that they don't fit. In a square-peg-round-hole relationship, one or both of you want the other person and your relationship to be someone or something it is not, and in some cases can never be. Typically, one or both of you want something out of the relationship that the other person either cannot or does not want to give.

Also, typically in these relationships, one or both of you wish that you could change something about the other person that can't be changed, can't be changed easily, or that the other person doesn't want to change. Here are some of the things people in square-peg-round-hole relationships might want the other person to be:

✓ Taller
✓ Shorter
✓ Younger
✓ Older
✓ Sexier
✓ Slimmer
✓ Smarter
✓ Better looking
✓ Better educated
✓ Richer

Sometimes people want to change things like the other person's personality; for example, wanting them to be more laid back and relaxed, or more assertive, or more outgoing, or communicative and so forth. Sometimes, also, one person wants to "fix" something in the other person. Fixing is a particularly tall order. It's hard enough to fix yourself; and as hard as that is, I'd say it's at least ten times harder to change—let alone fix—someone else. Not surprisingly, square-peg-round-hole relationships are often toxic to both people.

- What tends to keep these relationships going is that there are just enough plusses for both people to stay in the relationship. However, not many of these plusses are the ones that are the most important or truly desired, so as a result, there is often a chronic sense of unfulfillment and dissatisfaction on one or both sides.
- Like all relationships, square-peg-round-hole relationships start off optimistically enough. However, what starts out as optimism after a while can feel more and more like an illusion. When sooner or later it becomes obvious that nothing's going to change, illusion turns into disillusion,

and with it, comes deep disappointment, frustration, and resentment.

- Another reason these relationships are particularly conflict-prone is that for one or both people, full commitment to the relationship depends on the other person changing. Because the changes (or fixes) desired in the other person often range in difficulty from nearly impossible to impossible, commitment in these relationships often ranges from nearly zero to zero.

- Finally, one or both people are often reminded of what is missing for them in the other person; for example, when going out, noticing others, meeting others, learning about others, and so forth. To the person who wants the other to change, this can create a never-ending sense of frustration and even resentment. It can also lead to ambivalence, along with passive (and sometimes not so passive) aggressive outbursts (e.g., harsh words, constant belittling and criticism, as well as verbal and non-verbal messages that boil down to saying "You're not good enough...").

- For the person who's under pressure to change this can cause untold distress. It's frustrating, draining, doomed to failure and, sooner or later, as their resentment builds, sparks a backlash.

**One of the hardest things in the world
is to try to be someone you're not.**

When a square-peg-round-hole relationship ends, it's often said that it was never meant to be. True enough: Square pegs will never fit in round holes. What is also true is that it's too bad it can take one or both people so long to accept this simple truth.

4.6 LOP-SIDED RELATIONSHIPS

Because no one and no relationship is perfect, all relationships involve some degree of compromise, or plainly put, give and take on both sides. This is OK, of course, when the give and take is equal on both sides. However, in a lop-sided relationship, one person gives more than their fair share.

One important way of giving in the give-and-take of any relationship is to occasionally accommodate the other person's preferences, wants, or needs. ***In a lop-sided relationship, the person doing more of the giving is typically also <u>over-accommodating</u>.***

There are many reasons why lop-sided relationships are conflict prone. First, you may remember the point I made in Chapter 1: When it comes to relationship fairness, if you feel that you're the one who's been doing most of the giving or accommodating and have been making a much bigger effort to keep the relationship afloat, you'll feel short-changed and resentful sooner or later. Second, the feeling that you're "doing all the work" magnifies your psychological loss each time you give something or give up something to accommodate the other person. Third, if you're the one doing most of the giving and most of the accommodating, then it's also likely that you'll be doing most of the reaching out or inviting (and most of the time not getting much of a response back). This means that if you're in a lop-sided relationship, you're also likely to:

- Feel taken for granted—or taken advantage of.
- Feel neglected.
- Feel that you're neglecting yourself because you're giving too much—and giving up too many things.
- Resent it every time the other person refuses or doesn't offer to do something that you would have readily done for them.

- Feel ambivalent about the relationship, which on top of everything else, adds to the cost (and therefore the minuses) of the relationship for you.
- Draw on your emotional credit card... often.

Naturally, there are different degrees of lop-sidedness, but if someone is in a lop-sided relationship, there is a good chance that they're also more likely to:

- doubt themselves and assume they've done something "wrong" to offend or displease the other person (e.g., when they say or do something assertive or to stick up for themselves);
- do lots of big or little things to please the other person—often out of genuine thoughtfulness—but also often at least partly out of a desire to gain or keep the other person's liking or approval (or to make up for what they think they did "wrong");
- do these to please the other person, even if it's at undue tangible or psychological expense (e.g., outside their comfort zone);
- not say something after experiencing a loss caused by the other person (remember, if the other person never hears anything to the contrary, they often assume whatever they did is OK);
- come up with excuses for what the other person did;
- give in to the other person to escape the discomfort of being in a conflict with them (which the other person often interprets as "proof" that they are "right");
- tend to apologize even for things they don't really have to (which the other person interprets as even more "proof" that they are "right");

- if the other person has wronged them, accept their olive branch too soon and accept their apology without being 100% ready to do so; and,
- resort to passive aggression as a means of expressing their anger and frustration (which is not likely to help much and often only leaves them feeling even more frustrated, angry, and resentful than ever).

The cost of all the compromising someone does for someone else over the years adds up. Indeed, over-accommodating people who've been in lop-sided relationships for years can find themselves emotionally burnt to a crisp out of pent-up anger and resentment.

There can be many reasons why someone stays in a lop-sided relationship. One of the most common is a genuine desire to be connected (or stay connected) with the other person. Sometimes, one person has some hold over the other (e.g., their attractiveness, financial security or power, or status). Sometimes one person is naturally more dominant or bossy than the other. Also, rightly or wrongly, the over-accommodating person may feel they have few options or alternatives (i.e., they either feel stuck or are stuck).

There is a big difference between over-accommodating out of love versus fear.

Socialization and deeply held values (e.g., putting others first), can also be factors, as can a sense of duty or obligation. Wishful thinking can also play a role (e.g., "If I keep doing this, sooner or later, they'll come around..."), as can believing that they have no choice in the matter. As I said in Chapter 2, one of the most difficult things for anyone is to be in a relationship that they think they need more than they want.

One of the effects of having been in a long-term lop-sided romantic relationship is that even long after it's over, people understandably remain sensitive about anything that reminds them of giving too much or over-accommodating whoever they try to form a new romantic relationship with. In other words, even the slightest hint of there being such expectations on the other person's part can become a relationship flashpoint.

4.7 TROUBLING TRIADS: LOP-SIDED THREE-WAY RELATIONSHIPS

> *"Two's company, three's a crowd."*
>
> ENGLISH PROVERB
> DATING BACK TO THE 1600S

As we all can relate to, this saying refers to the idea that a third person is not welcome when two people want to be alone. It also reminds us that, although harmony among three is as important as harmony between two, harmony among three is harder to maintain.

Ideally in any three-way relationship, all three people like each other, but in a lop-sided situation, two of the three people don't get along. To illustrate, consider Christopher, Michael, and Ashley. Christopher and Michael like each other, and Christopher and Ashley like each other, but Ashley and Michael don't. This is a lop-sided three-way relationship because, naturally, it would be better if all three people—Michael, Ashley, and Christopher—liked one another. But is this a problem?

Whether this three-way lop-sided relationship is problematic depends on what, if anything, Christopher, Michael, and Ashley must do **_together_**. If the three of them never or hardly ever need to spend time together, there likely isn't much of a problem. Every time Christopher is with Michael, he simply must try to make sure Ashley's not around, and every time he's with Ashley, he must try make sure Michael's not around. Lop-sided? Yes. Problematic? In this case, not particularly.

But now consider another lop-sided three-way relationship: Let's say a young couple—Kimia and Aiden—have been dating for a year and are thinking of marrying. Kimia's parents, who are recent immigrants and want to hold on to their traditions and cultural practices, disapprove of Aiden, and are against their daughter marrying him. Is this a problem? Is it conflict-prone? Yes, on both counts. However, how things turn out will depend, among other things, on Kimia's relationship and bond with her parents, and how strongly she holds the values and norms of her family's culture.

Now consider the following lop-sided three-way relationship: Kyle and Mary—both in their late 30s—are in a budding romantic relationship and Mary's daughter Emma, develops a strong dislike for her potential stepparent. In this case let's say:

- Mary loves Kyle and Kyle loves Mary;
- Mary loves her ten-year-old daughter, Emma, and Emma loves her mom; but,
- Emma doesn't like Kyle at all.

Sound familiar? This kind of situation sometimes occurs in blended families. Clearly, in addition to the strained relationship between Emma and her mom's boyfriend, this troubling triad will be especially conflict-prone for Mary and Kyle. Why conflict-prone?

- First, it's hard to feel 100% positive about a person who is intensely disliked by someone you love. Second, it's also hard to feel 100% positive about a person who intensely dislikes someone you love.

- What this means is that, for Mary, it's going to be hard to be 100% positive about Kyle because of how her daughter feels about him. So, until Emma and Kyle can get along, there will always be some degree of reservation from Mary about Kyle. Moreover, if she detects the slightest animosity by Kyle toward Emma, it could be an instant deal breaker.

- In addition, as a potential new family, Mary, Kyle, and Emma could and should be doing lots of things together (from having dinner to going on vacations). But in this case doing anything together will be strained by resentments that are never far from the surface. At best, their time together will be incident-free. At worst, it will be full of disagreements and arguments, punctuated by the occasional blow up. Naturally, all this will add a lot to the cost of the relationship for both Mary and Kyle.

- There will be situations when Mary must make decisions that will either go Kyle's way or Emma's way. This will often leave Mary in a bind and feeling ambivalent (i.e., "I want Kyle to be happy when we're together, but I also want Emma to be happy when we're together."). Many of Mary's choices will boil down to siding with either Kyle or Emma (e.g., "Do we watch the movie Emma wants to see or the one Kyle wants to see?"). Either way, there's a good chance that someone won't be happy.

- If all this weren't bad enough, Mary may also be resentful of her daughter because of how she feels about Kyle, and Emma might be resentful of her mom for her choice of boyfriend. And, as for Kyle, well, he may feel at least a little resentful toward both.

- Finally, and this goes without saying, if Mary ever came

to feel that she must choose between keeping Kyle and staying close to her daughter, she is not likely to sacrifice her relationship with Emma for her relationship with Kyle. If it ever came to this, Mary and Kyle's relationship would likely end.

Clearly, the most obvious way for this conflict-prone relationship to change for the better would be for the relationship between Emma and Kyle to improve. Mary and Kyle may be able to work together to help make that happen with an awareness of what is going on among the three of them, and why. It is also possible that if the relationship between Mary and Kyle is strong enough, and if Emma senses this and sees that her mother is genuinely happy because of it, she might on her own initiative begin to change the way she feels about Kyle and acts towards him.

Generally, though, there are no simple rules for dealing with conflicts when three-way relationships are lop-sided. Furthermore, conflict resolution in these relationships is an uphill climb. This is especially so when one or both people have the option (however painful it may be) of exiting the relationship. When there is no easy option of exiting—and unless the animosity between the two conflicted people is resolved—the stage is often set for long-term, foundational conflict.

4.8 UNCHARTED TERRITORY RELATIONSHIPS

Change is an unavoidable part of our lives: Even if we don't go looking for change, more often than not it seems, change comes looking for us... Perhaps the most dramatic example of this in recent years is the upheaval caused around the world by the COVID-19 virus. Of course, unexpected change can also come as a welcomed surprise. On top of this, we often actively seek out change in our lives and want to make it happen.

Whether it brings joy or upheaval, people in all sorts of relationships—friendships, romantic relationships, business relationships or family—sooner or later face a change they've never faced before. In other words, all relationships, sooner or later, enter uncharted territory. Of course, many positive and creative things can come out of relationships in uncharted territory, so why is change potentially conflict-prone at all?

- First, change never occurs in isolation: We change relative to others; we can change because of or despite the expectations of others; and we can also change with or without the support of others. This can sometimes bring people into conflict.
- Second, your compatibility is put to the test when you enter uncharted territory with someone.

Many couples in the early stages of their relationship consider taking a trip together, and for good reason. Traveling can literally take you both into uncharted territory, which provides a chance to see how well you get along.

It's easy to see why lots of aspects of any relationship are put to the test when the change is unwanted and distressing, as when an illness or an accident befalls one or both of you. But change, even when it's exciting, can be stressful in its own way, for example:

- Getting into a relationship with someone whose background is completely different from yours, or anyone else's you've ever known.
- Moving in together.
- Marrying.
- Having a child together.

  ○ Moving to a new city together.
  ○ Moving to a new country together.
  ○ Starting a business together for the first time.
  ○ Trying to balance business and friendship and make it work.

Whether thrust upon both of you by circumstance, or actively sought out by both of you, and especially when the change you experience is sudden and dramatic, it's easy to lose your bearings. And during it all, you have to quickly learn to relate to one another in new ways, and maybe "unlearn" some old ways. So, what aspects of any relationship are put to the test when in uncharted territory?

- First, your compatibility in temperament, personality and communication is put to the test—not to mention your honesty and commitment.
- Second, your compatibility in values is put to the test. This is because it's easy to say to the other person that you value something (e.g., family over career) but it's only when a real opportunity arises (e.g., a great job offer that would involve frequent trips away from home) that what you said is truly tested.

Being in uncharted territory, and thus dealing with situations you've never been in before can be exciting, but it can also often take a lot out of both of you emotionally.

Although uncharted territory tests relationships, those relationships that pass such tests are strengthened. Indeed, the ability of any relationship you're in—whether personal or professional—to survive or even thrive—amid change can have lasting effects on the direction it takes and on the fulfillment it brings to both of you. In fact, just as surmounting change can transform ordinary people into extraordinary people, so too can ordinary relationships be transformed into extraordinary ones!

4.9 SOME CONCLUDING THOUGHTS ON CONFLICT-PRONE RELATIONSHIPS

There are a few important things to keep in mind about conflict-prone relationships:

- All of them have this in common: They can lead to endless and pointless arguments that go nowhere leaving frustration, anger, disappointment, and hurt in their wake. As you'll recall from Chapter 2, there is often a conflict behind the conflict when people argue often. Well, it's often the case that being in one of these conflict-prone relationships is the conflict behind the conflict.
- The different types of conflict-prone relationships are not necessarily mutually exclusive. There are often overlaps among them. For example, a lop-sided relationship can also be strained, draining, and ambivalent. A stretched relationship can also be in uncharted territory, or also be a square-peg-round-hole relationship. Can draining relationships also be ambivalent? Yes. After all, ambivalence is draining. Can a stretched relationship be draining? Yes, some aspects of relationship stretch can be draining. Can there be ambivalence in stretched relationships? Yes. Can stretched relationships also be lop-sided? They usually are.
- You can go from one kind of conflict-prone relationship to another with someone; for example, you can go from being stretched to ambivalent or from stretched to strained.

- As difficult as conflict-prone relationships can be, it's not all doom and gloom. Conflicts that don't end a relationship can make it stronger. Deciding whether you want to try to resolve a conflict is the topic of the next chapter—and, if you decide to go ahead and try to resolve it, Chapter 6 covers how to go about it.

Consider taking a few minutes to reflect on past or present conflict-prone relationships you've been in or are in. Which type of conflict-prone relationship–or combination of types–would you say best describe them? Did any of them start out being one type and morph into another?

Worksheets for this exercise are available from www.theconflictresolvingnetwork.com

DO YOU WANT TO RESOLVE THIS CONFLICT?

> *"Nothing is more difficult, and therefore more precious, than to be able to decide."*
>
> NAPOLEON BONAPARTE (1769–1821)

When two people want to resolve their conflict, most of the time they'll find a way to do it. Where there's a will, on both sides, there's usually a way. For most conflicts and most people—especially if it's a conflict between friends, romantic partners, or family members— "Do you want to resolve this conflict?" rarely needs to be asked outright. It's almost always an automatic yes.

This is a good thing because, usually, even just trying to resolve a conflict is also a good thing. After all, even if a conflict can't be fully resolved, it's possible to reduce its negative impact for all concerned. But resolving a conflict, especially a major one, can take a lot out of you. For example, it can take a lot of time, effort, and sometimes money, and can also involve some risk (i.e., wasted time possibly along with wasted effort and wasted money, if things don't work out). Then the question "Do you want to resolve this conflict?" is not as easy to answer. The purpose of this chapter is to help you find the answer to this all-important question whenever you need to.

It's sometimes hard to say whether you want to resolve a conflict or not because, among other things, you may not know if the conflict you're in can be resolved until you try. Sometimes too, it's the relationship itself that hangs in the balance. In this case, you're deciding whether to resolve the conflict and continue the relationship or end it and cut all ties. Although most of the time the future of a relationship is not in question, the decision whether to try to resolve the conflict can still be difficult. The relationship itself may not be at stake but its future quality might be.

Although it may strike you as odd to read this in a book devoted to conflict resolution, I'll say there are some conflicts that should probably never be resolved, and where all ties should be cut. ***Sometimes, just as there are conflicts worth walking away from, there are relationships worth walking away from.*** While I can't tell you which relationships you should walk away from and which ones you should hold onto, I can suggest questions to ask yourself to help you make that decision for yourself.

Over the years, I've found that one of the best things I can do to help people decide whether or not to resolve a conflict is to ask them carefully chosen questions that help them focus their thoughts. ***This chapter does just that: It asks questions that help you think through whether to try to resolve a conflict or not, whatever the stakes may be.***

The questions I have for you are built on the tried-and-true strategy of drawing up a list of "pros" and "cons," but with four added considerations I believe are critical to helping you make the best possible decision. They are:

- First, and above all, remember that in most situations, there are both good and bad things that can come from resolving any conflict as well as good and bad things that can come from *not* resolving it. So, always ask yourself what the pros are (i.e., the benefits or plusses) as well as what the cons are (i.e., the costs or minuses) of *both* options. Generally speaking, both options (i.e., "Yes, try to resolve" versus "No, don't") should be on the table.

> *"To give an authentic 'yes' you have to be able to give an authentic 'no.'"*
> EDWIN L. HERSCH, M.D.
> CANADIAN PSYCHIATRIST

- Second, always consider the costs and benefits of both "yes" and "no" not just for yourself, but also for those who matter to you the most (e.g., your spouse, romantic partner, children, parents, other family members, best friends, bosses, business partners, etc.). Being in a serious conflict and trying to decide what to do about it can be so emotionally charged and consuming that it's sometimes easy to overlook how your decision might affect others—including those closest to you.

> *"You don't love someone for their looks, or their clothes, or for their fancy car, but because they sing a song only you can hear"*
> OSCAR WILDE
> IRISH WRITER (1854–1900)

- Third, ask yourself ***how much*** each one of the costs and benefits of both "yes" and "no" could mean to you (and those closest to you). Counting the number of plusses and minuses is what a lot of people do when they draw up a list of pros and cons. However, not all plusses and minuses matter the same amount or in the same way. *As I mentioned in Chapter 4, one minus can outweigh a dozen plusses (or for that matter, all of them), and one plus can outweigh a dozen minuses... or all of them.*

If there's one really great thing about a relationship and if it means enough to you, it can make you not care all that much about any of the not-so-great things. Simply put, one plus can outweigh all minuses, as well as the other way around.

- Lastly, although it's perfectly natural to think mainly of those plusses and minuses that are likely to come right away, it's often just as important to ask yourself: "What could happen—both good and bad—in the months or even years from now if I resolve this conflict; and, what might happen if I don't?" In other words, it can be important to look beyond the short term and imagine what the future could look like if things work out as you would like them to, as well as what things might look like if they don't.

↓ **Worksheets for this chapter are available from www.theconflictresolvingnetwork.com**

5.1 OVERVIEW OF THE QUESTIONS TO ASK YOURSELF

There are many things to consider when deciding between resolving a conflict or not; and even more so if you're also wondering if you should stay in a relationship or not. However, in either case, they all come down to these three interconnected, big-picture questions: What are the *plusses or benefits—tangible and psychological—* of both options? What are the *minuses or costs—tangible and psychological—* of both options? What might the *future* look like with both options?

Benefits
Tangible *and* Psychological

Costs
Tangible *and* Psychological

The Future?

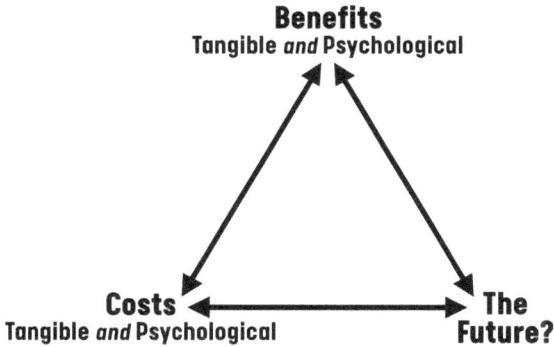

These three points form a triangle and provide a handy way of organizing your thoughts. Before going on to the decision-guiding questions themselves, let me give you an overview of what each point of the triangle covers.

As well as asking yourself these questions to help you decide about a current conflict, you can also use them to take another look at past decisions.

5.1.1 TANGIBLE COSTS AND BENEFITS

As you may recall from Chapter 1, the minuses of any relationship (and what you lose as a result and what that costs you) can be tangible or psychological. By extension, relationship plusses or benefits can be tangible or psychological too. In a nutshell then, there can be both tangible and psychological costs and benefits of both resolving a conflict as well as choosing not to resolve it.

Tangible Costs

- Tangible costs (or losses) include the loss of money or personal property, as well as time. Tangible costs include having to spend money or having to forgo—or do without—money that you need, want, or believe you deserve. Possessions damaged, lost, taken, or stolen are all tangible costs as is time spent, lost, or wasted (e.g., the time and money it takes to repair what's been damaged or to get back what was taken from you). Physical injury or a downturn in your health—or the health of someone close to you—are also tangible costs.

- Tangible costs can also be having to give up all or some of whatever you've already spent or invested in a relationship, or jointly built and own.

- As I mentioned in Chapter 1, someone taking away, or denying or not telling you about a chance at something (e.g., not being told about a job opening) or not receiving money or property you're entitled to all have a tangible cost.

- Opportunity cost is another cost, and one that people often overlook. The cost of a lost opportunity can be tangible or psychological. Opportunity cost refers to the benefits you give up by choosing one option over another. For example, let's say you decide to resolve a conflict with Person A. One of the tangible opportunity costs in this case is giving up whatever benefits you could have had spending the same amount of time and money on something—or someone—else.

When thinking of tangible costs, try to picture what the impact would be of having less time or money to spend with someone special to you, or on for example, something you love, want, or need to do.

Tangible Benefits

- Tangible benefits include having more money (whether it's money saved or earned), acquiring things like property or possessions, or in some cases, being able to keep the things you have. Simply put, tangible benefits often mean being better off financially. Tangible benefits can also be conveniences and things that free up time for you. Finally, an improvement in your health, or in the health of someone close to you are also tangible benefits.

When thinking about tangible benefits, such as more money or time, try to picture it in real life; for example, what it would be like to have that money and time to spend either on or with someone special, or on something important to you.

5.1.2 PSYCHOLOGICAL COSTS AND BENEFITS

Psychological Costs

- As you may also remember from Chapter 1, psychological loss refers to the emotional cost to you of what someone has done. Psychological costs are the flashpoint feelings such as frustration, disappointment, resentment and hurt or fear you endure because of what someone else did. Similarly, ambivalence (discussed in the previous chapter) along with worry about how things might turn out, are also psychological costs. As I also mentioned in Chapter 1, in addition to the emotional toll such feelings take, psychological cost also refers to the cost to you in mental energy of having to cope with, fight or suppress such feelings—which can be exhausting.

- In addition to giving up what you've tangibly invested in a relationship, having to say goodbye to whatever you've emotionally invested in it can have a heavy psychological cost. ***Whether tangible or psychological, it's hard to cut your losses!***

- Psychological costs also come from social consequences such as increased conflict with some people (especially those closest to you). Rejection, being snubbed, or losing a friend can also take a heavy psychological toll.

- Just as there are tangible opportunity costs, there are psychological opportunity costs. Like FOMO—the Fear of Missing Out—one potential cost of staying in a relationship that you have some doubts about, are niggling questions such as "Who could I be with instead?", "What could I be doing instead?", and "Could I do better?"

  ○ This is one of the reasons why, as I noted in the previous chapter, you can be tempted to have a "Plan B" when you're feeling ambivalent about someone. This often involves either holding off on making any further commitment in case someone better (i.e., a better match or a better "catch") comes along, or actively looking for someone better (e.g., on social media or an online dating site).

Note that there can be both psychological and tangible costs to maintaining a "Plan B" behind someone's back. For example, your psychological costs can include feeling guilty (for as long as you're not caught) and mortified (if you are).

- Not only are flashpoint feelings (e.g., frustration, disappointment, resentment) psychological costs, but so is the ***effort*** it takes to cope with them:
  - No matter how you cut it, being in conflict can take a lot out of you emotionally. For example, it can take a lot of effort to cope with the flashpoints that either started your conflict, are the result of it, or are keeping it going. It also takes a lot of time and effort too to recover from frequent, and emotionally draining, fights, blow ups and so forth...

As I mentioned in Chapter 2, the build-up of conflict fatigue is often one of the things that either drives people further apart or compels them, sooner or later, to try to make peace.

  - It can also take a lot of effort to get your conflict resolved and abide by whatever changes you must ake for the relationship to work (e.g., compromising).
  - Now, the thing is that ***how much*** effort something takes depends on a lot of factors. What might be easy for one person, may take a lot more effort for someone else. Why?
    - First, regardless of whatever skill, talent, and experience you have, any form of exertion (physical, intellectual, or emotional), takes willpower. And, as anyone who's ever dieted, quit smoking, or tried to keep a New Year's resolution knows, willpower can run low—or just run out—after a while.
    - Second, as you may remember from Chapter 4, the more things you have on your plate (e.g.,

children, a long commute, a demanding job, being on a tight budget), the more willpower you will need to draw on throughout your day.

- The more willpower you must draw upon on any given day, the more likely you'll feel tapped out as the days, weeks and months go on. As your willpower dwindles, the more effort everything seems to take. In fact, ***the perceived effort to do anything often goes up dramatically with the number of items on your plate!***

- What does this mean? Well, among other things, it means that with a lot going on in your life already, the effort it will take to resolve a conflict can seem—rightly or wrongly—to be a lot to ask. Maybe even too much. Furthermore, whatever effort you may have to make by way of compromising or accommodating to keep the conflict resolved might also seem to be a lot to ask.

Someone who doesn't know or appreciate what you've got on your plate may not understand your decision—or why you can't make one just yet. Why? Because what looks like an easy decision to them is actually a lot harder for you to make than they can possibly imagine!

In situations like this, I'd advise you to always consider telling the other person what is going on—don't leave them wondering. Don't just "disappear."

- There is one last psychological cost related to effort worth noting, and that is the emotional cost of acting on your decision. This can be the case, whatever your decision is—whether to offer an olive branch or not, to apologize or not, to have that tough and awkward conversation or not, or whether to actually say goodbye.

Sometimes acting on a decision can be just as hard as coming to it.

Psychological Benefits

- Psychological benefits are the good feelings (e.g., fireworks feelings such as elation, joy, and contentment) that you can have in any relationship regardless of what kind of relationship it is (if you haven't yet, try the fireworks feelings exercise in Chapter 3). Rekindling relationship fireworks, or adding new ones, typically tops most people's reasons for wanting to resolve a conflict.
- Psychological benefits can also come from improvements in your social life. For example, making new friends, becoming closer to someone special to you, and restoring or repairing important relationships all have psychological benefits. Earning the approval, praise, admiration, or respect of people who matter to you also has psychological benefits.
- Lastly, another commonly felt psychological benefit comes from getting something off your chest, clearing the air, and feeling better for having done so. Sometimes, as noted in Chapter 2, simply saying something you feel strongly about, but have bottled up for a long time feels good when it's finally said.

One Last Point about Tangible or Psychological Benefits

- If you've ever taken something to relieve a headache, you'll know it's a good thing when something bad goes away. So, anything (whether tangible or psychological) that **stops or prevents** something bad from happening is a plus that can benefit you tangibly or psychologically (e.g., the feeling of relief when something stops the emotional stress of a conflict).

Always remember that you can experience a psychological benefit (or cost) without there being anything tangible behind it, as when someone tells you how much they like you or what a fantastic person you are. But rarely do tangible costs or benefits come your way without there being some psychological costs or benefits along with them.

5.1.3 THE FUTURE

You can't always predict the future, but you can picture it.

The future is not a concern in every relationship; indeed, many relationships run perfectly well on a one-day-at-a-time basis. But if you've ever been in a relationship where you felt the need to pause and ask yourself "Where's this going?" or "Where could this go?" you'll appreciate just how important thinking about the future can be.

- So, as I noted earlier, along with thinking about the immediate benefits and costs to resolving or not resolving a conflict, it's sometimes a good idea to imagine what your future might look like in the months or even years ahead following either decision.
- Second, consider what the **odds** are of both good and bad things happening—sooner or later—with either decision. How sure or confident are you that the good things you expect or hope to happen will happen? What are the chances that the bad things will happen?
- The third aspect of the future to consider is what the **_impact_** would be if any of the good or bad things that could happen actually happened because of your decision. *While the odds you give of something—good or bad—happening is one thing, how big an impact it would have—good or bad on your life, and the lives of those closest to you—is quite another! Basically, this is taking into consideration how high the stakes are.*
- Finally, consider how long a benefit or cost will likely last. Some costs are short-lived, as are some benefits. Consider too that with some decisions the costs are very short-lived, but the benefits can last a lifetime.

Sometimes, speaking out and enduring a few minutes of awkwardness and discomfort can save you—and maybe many others in your life—years of unhappiness, conflict, and grief. It is also true that resisting the temptation to do something you'd really like to in the heat of the moment can do the same.

Comparing possible futures—especially when the immediate costs and benefits of both options are about equal—can often tip the scales in favor of one decision or the other.

5.2 HOW TO GET THE MOST OUT OF THE
DECISION-GUIDING QUESTIONS

The questions I have for you may help you consider things that would not ordinarily come to mind and can also be a springboard to further questions. Indeed, I've found that people typically come up with many additional and helpful questions specific to their situation, relationship, and the conflict they are in.

To be clear, here is what I mean by choosing "Yes" versus "No:" Choosing "Yes" means deciding to try to resolve the conflict; and, if need be, rearranging the relationship (or at least compromising somewhat) to resolve it. Choosing "No" can mean deciding not to resolve the conflict by not saying or doing anything; or deciding not to resolve it (or to finally stop trying) by leaving the relationship, cutting all ties, and perhaps never seeing the other person again.

You can organize your thoughts using two decision-guiding triangles shown on the next page. One represents the costs, benefits, and future of "Yes" and the other, the costs, benefits, and future of "No."

Before you begin, allow me to share some suggestions on how you can get the most out of these questions.

- I'm assuming that if you're going through these questions, you have a specific conflict in mind and a decision to make about it. If so, give some thought to the following:
  - Would you include the person with whom you're having this conflict among those who mean the most to you?
  - Do you feel any obligation or duty to try and resolve your conflict? How about the other person?
  - Do you owe the other person anything? By this I mean, for example, were they at some point gracious, understanding or forgiving toward you when you did something wrong? Did they cut you some slack? Do you feel that now might be your chance to return the favor?

Decision-Guiding Triangles

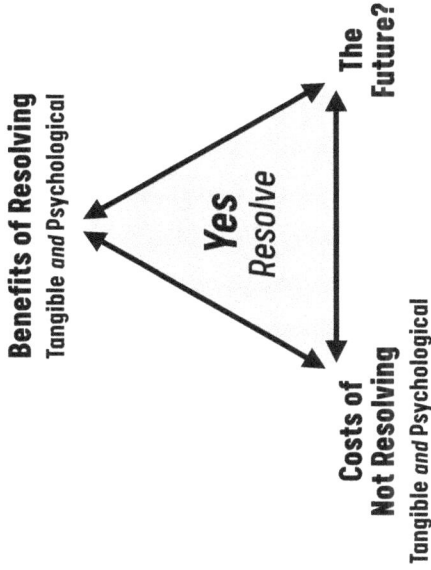

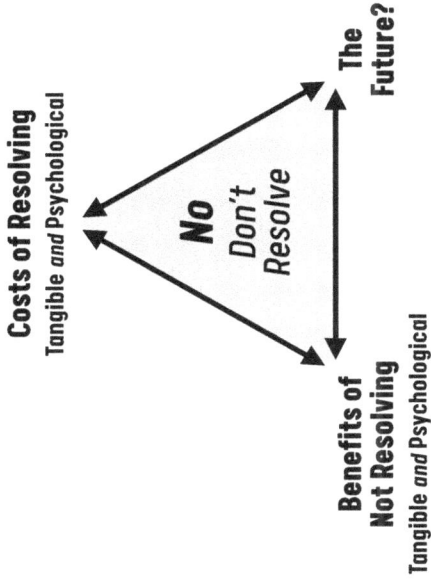

Benefits of Resolving
Tangible *and* Psychological

The Future?

Yes
Resolve

Costs of Not Resolving
Tangible *and* Psychological

Costs of Resolving
Tangible *and* Psychological

The Future?

No
Don't Resolve

Benefits of Not Resolving
Tangible *and* Psychological

    ◦   Is leaving this relationship even an option? If so, is it something you are considering now? Is it something you would do only as a last resort?

- Be honest with yourself. Some questions, like those above —as well as many of the ones to follow—are likely to take some soul searching.
- As you go through the questions, don't rush. The answers to some of them might take a while to think through. Give yourself as much time as you need to mull things over.
- You might also find it helpful to ask someone you trust to be your sounding board so you can think out loud, or simply kick ideas around and brainstorm together.

Sometimes how you really think and feel deep down inside has to be said to someone out loud, and not just in your head for it to truly register with you. There's something about someone bearing witness to what you say that makes all the difference. I'm sure you've had moments in your life when, as you talked to your closest and most trusted friend about something that was troubling you, you unexpectedly found yourself saying out loud something–a secret, a truth, a feeling–that up until then you hadn't dared admit, even to yourself.

One last thing: As you work through these questions, you'll find that you'll go back and forth between "yes" and "no" just as you do when you're feeling ambivalent about someone. The good news is that, as you continue to think through your answers, clarity and focus will start to emerge. In fact, what often happens is that sooner or later something (like a benefit or a cost or a future consideration) occurs to you that tips the balance, and finally your decision becomes clear. So, without further ado, here are the questions I have for you.

5.3 THE BENEFITS, COSTS AND FUTURE OF RESOLVING YOUR CONFLICT: THE "YES, RESOLVE" TRIANGLE

This first set of questions asks you about the likely and immediate tangible and psychological benefits of resolving your conflict. The second section asks what the future might look like in the months and years ahead if you resolved your conflict. In other words, I'd like you to reflect on the tangible and psychological plusses of your relationship, and the good things and benefits that could come both right away and in the future if you resolve your conflict.

5.3.1 QUESTIONS ABOUT THE IMMEDIATE BENEFITS OF RESOLVING YOUR CONFLICT

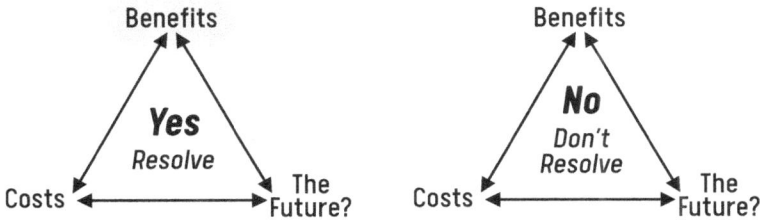

What Would the Likely Immediate <u>Tangible</u> Benefits Be for You and Those Who Matter to You the Most if You Resolved this Conflict?

1. Are there any good things with tangible benefits that are likely to happen right away, or soon after you resolve your conflict? If so, would these benefits be connected to money or possessions? Time? Convenience? Health?
2. Would resolving this conflict stop anything bad from happening? For example, would it prevent losing some important possessions or property or prevent some tangible

expense such as paying a financial settlement? Would it stop or prevent the dissolution of a business, or prevent having to stop some joint endeavor or opportunity from developing (e.g., pursuing a new job, a new career, or furthering your education)?

3. Would you and those closest to you likely be better off right away or soon after resolving this conflict, compared to where you'd be if you didn't resolve it? If not better off, would you at least not be worse off?

4. If you would be better off, how much better off? How likely is that?

What Would the Likely Immediate _Psychological Benefits_ Be for You and Those Who Matter to You the Most if you Resolved this Conflict?

1. If you think you'd likely be as well or better off with your conflict resolved, which psychological benefits could or would come with that? Think for a moment of those tangibles that bring comfort, safety, or enjoyment to your life. For example, if you resolved your conflict, what tangible support or help could you continue to count on? What things would you not have to worry about? How big an impact would these tangibles have on your lifestyle and well-being and the lifestyle and well-being of those closest to you?

2. In addition to the impact of any of the tangible benefits that are likely to materialize, would it also feel good to get the resolution of this conflict started? For example:

    •   How good would it feel to get something off your chest, clear the air, or simply say something about what is bothering you?

- And, if you feel at least partly responsible for starting the conflict, how good would it feel to admit to it, apologize, and get that off your chest?

For the rest of these questions, I'd like you to focus on as many of the fireworks or psychological plusses of your relationship as you can. Once again, if you haven't already, consider doing the "Putting Your Relationship Fireworks and Flashpoints into Words" exercise in Chapter 3.

---

3. Is the other person someone who brings fireworks into your life that no one else can? Does the other person bring out the best in you in a way that no one else can? If you resolved your conflict would all this likely return? Could it even be furthered and enhanced as a result?

4. Having resolved your conflict, would the two of you likely become closer than you were before? Could your bond become stronger and deeper? Would there likely be other positive changes in your relationship because you resolved your conflict?

5. Could you learn something valuable from having resolved this conflict? If so, would it likely in some ways make you, for example: A better person? A better partner? Parent? Friend? Could it make you a stronger couple? A closer family? In what ways?

6. Are there things about yourself that you want to improve or change that resolving this conflict would motivate you to do, or help you achieve?

7. If you had to rearrange your relationship, how likely is it that you would keep all the fireworks you have on your relationship menu?

8. If you couldn't keep all the fireworks you once had in your relationship, how likely is it that you could keep the ones you most want to keep? If you could keep them, how much would that mean to you?

9. Could you make any new fireworks together if you resolved your conflict?

10. Is it likely that you could keep the friends you want to keep if you resolved this conflict?

11. Is it likely you could make new friends and broaden your social network?

12. Could you gain the approval, praise, admiration, or respect of people who matter to you?

13. Is there someone or are there people you'd likely be closer to if you resolved this conflict?

14. Are there any relationships that you can think of that could likely be restored or repaired because you resolved this conflict?

15. Would resolving this conflict stop or prevent a problem, or prevent something that already is a problem from getting worse? For example:
    - How much distress caused by the conflict itself would end right away if it were resolved?
    - Which minuses or flashpoints in your relationship could be fixed right away or soon after?
    - Which flashpoints, even if not fixed completely, might be less troubling or happen less often?

16. Reflecting on these good things, which ones are the most likely to happen? Least likely? Which good things matter to you and those closest to you the most? The least?

5.3.2 QUESTIONS ABOUT THE POSSIBLE FUTURE BENEFITS OF RESOLVING YOUR CONFLICT

The next questions are to help get you thinking about what future potential you see in your relationship and the upside that resolving your conflict could bring you and those who matter to you the most. But first let me ask you this: ***How confident are you that the two of you can resolve your conflict if you try?***

There are many things that can influence the likelihood of a conflict being resolved. Although every situation is different, generally, the outlook for the successful resolution of most conflicts (or at least a "softer landing") is when:

✓ Both of you want to resolve your conflict.

✓ The two of you have a track record of successfully resolving your conflicts (this is a _big_ plus!).

✓ When you do have conflicts, it doesn't take much, and it doesn't take long, to get over them and patch things up.

✓ You both know and agree on the nature of your relationship and have a pretty good idea about what each of you wants from it.

✓ Neither of you are "maxed out" on your emotional credit card.

✓ There's still at least some love or liking, mutual respect, or loyalty between you (as well as attraction if it's a romantic relationship). In other words, your "positivity account" is not overdrawn. Why is this important?

Well, just as fireworks are the glue that holds many relationships together, it's love, liking, loyalty, trust, mutual respect, etc. that often get people through the toughest moments of resolving a conflict. As I mentioned in Chapter 2, it's often your positivity account with someone that opens the door to communication—and holds it open—when you need it most.

✓ One last thing worth mentioning that bodes well is this: If you both still think of yourselves in terms of "us" or "we" regardless how serious the conflict is you're having.

Resolving your conflict will likely be more challenging if:

✓ Your relationship is lop-sided and one of you is less eager to resolve your conflict than the other, or if you're in one or more of the other seven conflict-prone relationships; that is, strained, draining, ambivalent, stretched, square-peg-round-hole, three-way lop-sided, or uncharted territory.

✓ Your relationship is new and some big relationship flashpoints have already been triggered by one or both of you. Note too that if your relationship is new, it's also likely that you haven't had a chance to add much to your positivity account.

✓ You've known each other for years and the conflict has been going on for years (in which case, it might be foundational in nature).

✓ You're both reaching the limit of your emotional credit card.

✓ Whether you've known each other for just a few weeks or many years, the outlook is not good if you don't know each other very well. How can it be that you've known each other for years yet you don't know each other well? This can happen when one of you has changed while the other has not; or if both of you have changed but in different ways and in opposite directions.

✓ If one of you doesn't trust the other, or if neither of you trust the other fully, the resolution of any conflict you have will be seriously impaired. When trust is low, even if you can communicate, it's hard to believe anything the other person says. ***Communication without trust goes nowhere and trust without communication doesn't take you far enough.***

✓ If your conflicts have gradually increased in how often they occur, how intense they are and how long they last, then (as I mentioned earlier), this is often a sign that there is a deeper, underlying conflict going on; that is to say, a conflict behind the conflict.

If you're not sure you'll be able to resolve your conflict, consider reading Chapter 6 if you haven't already. Chapter 6 covers what you need to know and do to navigate the conflict resolution process, which should give you a better sense of what the chances are of the two of you being able to resolve your conflict. Alternatively, simply completing the rest of the decision-guiding questions will give you a clearer idea of how doable the resolution of your conflict might be.

How Good Could the Future Be for You and Those Who Matter to You the Most if You Resolved Your Conflict?

Possible Future Tangible Benefits

17. In addition to any of the good things with tangible benefits that are likely to happen right away if you resolve your conflict, are there other good things that could happen months or even years from now?

18. Would any of these tangible benefits of resolving your conflict be permanent and therefore could be passed on or shared with those who mean the most to you (e.g., your children)? Of those benefits that are not permanent, how long would they last?

19. Could additional opportunities (e.g., business, career, education) open up for you and those closest to you, if you resolve your conflict?

20. If you were to be as well or better off soon after having resolved this conflict, could things improve even further over time? If so, how likely is this to happen and what would be the impact on you and those you care about the most if it did?

Possible Future Psychological Benefits

1. Is this a chance to nip this conflict in the bud?

2. If the two of you *tried* but could not resolve your conflict, how likely is it that, together, you could nonetheless pave the way for a softer landing? For example, could you still be friends, or if not, then on friendly (or at least speaking) terms?

3. If you were to go your separate ways, could you do so with less bitterness between the two of you than if you had not tried to resolve your conflict?

4. If you did resolve your conflict are there other psychological benefits that could materialize in the months or years ahead? If so, what could they be?

5. How long would these additional benefits last? Which ones would last longest? How much would these mean to you? How much of an impact could these benefits have on your lifestyle and well-being? On the lifestyle and well-being of those who matter to you the most?

6. Would resolving your conflict depend on **_you_** changing? What would you have to change about yourself? How confident are you that you could change enough? Soon enough?

7. How much do you think resolving your conflict would depend on **_the other person_** changing? What would have to change? How confident are you that they could change enough and soon enough?

8. If you resolved your conflict and were on friendly terms with the other person, could this develop into a closer relationship at some point?

9. Bearing in mind how far away in the future some of these benefits may be, would they be worth the wait? Which ones would be worth waiting for?

10. Reflecting on these good things, which ones are the most likely to happen? Less likely? Which matter the most to you and those closest to you?

11. What are the two or three best things that could happen and that also have a pretty good chance of happening if you resolved your conflict? If these things did happen, how much would it mean to you and those who matter to you the most?

12. Speaking of the best things that could happen if you resolved your conflict, are any of these "longshots?" In other words, is it the prospect that at least one of them may happen that, although not very likely, still gives you some hope of a better relationship in the future? If so, what are they?

13. At the very least, setting aside what may or may not happen in the future, could resolving your conflict be a chance for the two of you to make a fresh start?

Decision Check-in #1

HOW ARE YOU LEANING?

✓   Are there enough positives in your relationship as it stands for you to want to resolve this conflict or not? Are these positives important enough to you and those closest to you? Are you confident enough that the good things you see coming from resolving your conflict will happen? *Plainly speaking, is there enough in it for you to make it worth your while to at least try to resolve your conflict?*

Note that in ordinary language when we say something's not worth it, what we're really saying is that the effort we think we'd need to make isn't worth what we expect to get, or that we're not sure that even if we made the effort, we'd get what we want.

✓   Let's say your answer is: "Yes, I want to resolve this conflict." Well, even if you're sure, it's only fair to yourself (and those closest to you) that you take some time to think about what negatives there might be (if any) of this decision. *In other words, while it's great that you want to resolve this conflict, now is a good time to ask yourself: At what cost?*

5.3.3 QUESTIONS ABOUT THE IMMEDIATE COSTS OF RESOLVING YOUR CONFLICT

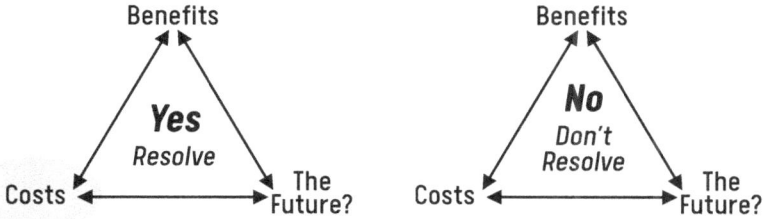

Resolving a conflict—especially one that's been going on for a long time—is never easy and often has costs. Take, for example, having to compromise. Whatever compromise you reach may not be perfect. You may not get everything you want and there may be things you wish you could have that are no longer on your relationship menu. There may be tangible and psychological plusses that you now can't have and minuses you wish you didn't have to accept but are nonetheless trade-offs necessary for a lasting resolution. Simply put, there are often both immediate and future tangible and psychological costs to resolving most conflicts.

What Would the Likely Immediate Tangible Costs Be for You and Those Who Matter to You the Most if you Resolved Your Conflict?

1.   Are there any bad things with tangible costs (e.g., in terms of time, money or health) that are likely to happen right away because you resolved your conflict? For example:
     • Could there be some financial reparation or penalty that you would have to pay for this conflict to be over?
     • Could there be a cost, such as professional fees, to resolving this conflict or to reaching some kind of agreement or settlement?

- Would you have to continue with some financial obligation or responsibility if you resolved this conflict?
- Would you likely have to take on some **_new_** financial obligation or responsibility if you resolved this conflict?
- Is there something good, tangibly speaking, that you wouldn't be able to get or keep because you resolved this conflict?

2. Is there anything about the relationship that is or could be a time-consuming inconvenience, and would it continue if your conflict were resolved?
3. Could there be an immediate tangible opportunity cost to resolving this conflict? By this I mean could the time and money you'd likely spend resolving it (and keeping this relationship going) be better spent on something (or someone) else?
4. All in all, would you and those closest to you be worse off (moneywise, timewise or health wise), sooner than later, if you resolved this conflict? If so, by how much?

What Would the Likely Immediate <u>Psychological</u> Costs Be for You and Those Who Matter to You the Most if You Resolved this Conflict?

1. If you think you'd likely be worse off (moneywise, timewise or health wise) if you resolved your conflict, what would this cost you psychologically? How about those closest to you? For example: What possessions would you miss? What creature comforts would you miss?
2. In addition to the psychological impact of any tangible costs there could be to resolving your conflict, could

there be any psychological costs for you to get the resolution of your conflict started? Would you have to do something that's hard for you? For example, would you have to swallow your pride in order to offer an olive branch or apologize?

3. Are you unsure whether the other person wants to resolve your conflict? Would it be hard for you to hear a "no" to your invitation to resolve it (e.g., your olive branch offering)? How likely do you think it is that you would hear a "no" right away?

4. To resolve your conflict—and keep it resolved—what psychological costs could there likely be for you and for those closest to you? For example:

   - How likely is it that you would have to rearrange your relationship to resolve this conflict? If it's likely that you would (and therefore must change what's on your relationship menu), which fireworks do you think would be off the menu right away?

   - What compromises or sacrifices would you likely have to make?

   - Would you probably have to give up doing things that you like or love to do?

   - Is there an important part of you that you'd likely have to deny or shut down?

   - Are there friendships you would have to end? Or be expected to end?

   - Is there one particularly close relationship—or a budding one—that you would likely have to end (for example, someone you'd have to break up with) for this conflict to be resolved?

   - In other words, are there friendships (budding or not) that you'd have to sacrifice?

   - Would you likely be discouraged from making new friends, or unable to make new friends?

- If you had to compromise, and you couldn't get everything you wanted, what relationship flashpoints would you likely continue to have to put up with?
- How likely is it that there are things you'd feel obligated to continue—or must continue—doing that you don't want to do?
- How about having to do new things? Are there new things the other person would likely want of you that you might not want to do?
- How difficult would it be to put up with or do any of these things? What if demands to do these things started to increase?

Questions such as these are important to consider, especially if you're in the disengagement stage of a conflict. When in disengagement, with bad feelings gradually fading and fond memories returning, it's easy to forget about the minuses of your relationship–which in some cases–are the very things that started your conflict in the first place.

---

5. What weaknesses, challenges, or problems of the other person's would you likely have to deal with again if you resolved this conflict? Could there be any new ones?

6. Are there people in the other person's life who are draining to be with and who you would have to continue being around? How often would this happen?

7. Is there anyone who matters to you who would be upset (e.g., deeply hurt, angered, or disappointed) if you resolved your conflict? How distressing would that be for you and those who matter to you the most?

8. If there are people who would be upset that you resolved your conflict, how likely is it that they would act

differently toward you (e.g., snub you)? How would they act toward those closest to you? How distressing would this be?

9. Could some important relationships be damaged or end if you resolved your conflict? How likely is it that conflicts would start with these people? How much of a strain would this be?

10. Is there something about yourself that could change in a bad way if you resolved this conflict? For example, could you slip back into some past bad habit if you resolved this conflict?

11. Are there any things that you would have to keep secret or lie about to resolve this conflict and keep it resolved? Who would you have to lie to or keep something from? How hard would it be to keep these secrets from being found out? How much effort would that take and how much would it cost you emotionally to keep this deception going?

12. Would you also have to lie to yourself?

13. Would you have to change to resolve your conflict and keep it resolved? How much effort do you think it would take for you to change, or be accommodating, to make this relationship work?

14. How difficult would making such sacrifices be for you? Would those sacrifices affect those closest to you? Would they have to make sacrifices too?

15. How much do you already have on your plate?

16. How much effort could, or can you, put into both resolving this conflict and keeping it resolved? For how long?

17. All in all, how much effort do you think it would take to resolve your conflict and keep it resolved?

18. Is there someone else you could be with who might be a better match? Is there something else you could be doing with all the effort you'd have to put into resolving this conflict and keeping this relationship alive that might be

more rewarding for you? In other words, is there a psychological opportunity cost to resolving this conflict?

19. Is there anything about this decision that would go against your values or conscience?

5.3.4 QUESTIONS ABOUT THE POSSIBLE FUTURE COSTS OF RESOLVING YOUR CONFLICT

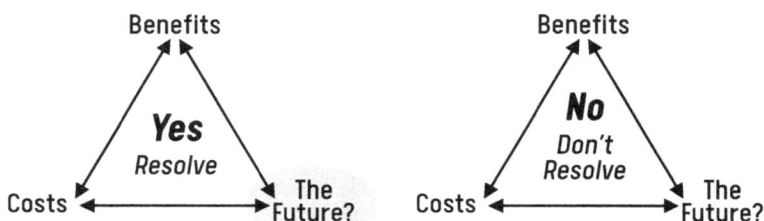

How Bad Could Things Get for You and Those Who Matter to You the Most if You Resolved Your Conflict?

Possible Future Tangible Costs

1. In addition to any bad things with tangible costs that are likely to happen right away if you resolved your conflict, are there any that could happen months or even years from now? How likely are any of them to happen?

2. Would any of these tangible costs of resolving your conflict be permanent (or at least outlive you) and therefore be a burden to others, such as your children? Of those tangible costs that are not permanent, how long would these last?

3. How long would it take to recover, for example financially or health-wise, from any of the bad things that could happen from resolving your conflict? How confident are you that you could recover?

4. Are there any opportunities that could be missed because you resolved your conflict? For example, would it be impossible or a lot harder to start a new job, or a business, pursue a new career or further your education?

5. In addition to what it might cost financially to resolve your conflict, would it continue to cost something extra to keep it resolved and for this relationship to continue? Is it possible that this relationship could cost you more than it did before? How much more? Would it be worth it?

6. If you were to be worse off soon after having resolved this conflict, could it worsen over time? If so, how likely is this to happen and what would the impact be on you and those you care about the most if it did?

7. If there were inconveniences that would likely continue if you resolved your conflict, could these grow as time goes on?

Possible Future Psychological Costs

1. Turning now to the possible future psychological costs of resolving your conflict, how likely is it that even trying to resolve it could make things worse? Is it worth taking the risk?

2. How long do you think it would take to recover emotionally from any of the likely immediate tangible or psychological costs of resolving your conflict? How confident are you that you could do so? How about those closest to you?

3. If resolving your conflict depends on the other person changing, what could happen if they don't?

4. If you had to compromise, and you couldn't get everything you wanted, of the flashpoints you'd likely have to continue to put up with:
   - Could any of them get worse?
   - Could any new flashpoints pop up?

- What if there were more and they started to add up?
- What fireworks might you be missing, and for how long?

5. If you had to keep certain things a secret to resolve your conflict or keep it resolved, how likely is it that sooner or later the truth would come out?

6. Would there be others who know the truth and you'd need to count on to keep your secret? Would they have as much to lose as you if the secret got out? If not, how much could you trust them to keep your secret? Even if you trusted them, how much could you count on them to never accidentally let your secret out?

7. What would happen if you were found out? How hard would that be on you and those who matter to you the most?

8. Setting aside all that you would have to do to keep the peace with the other person, and the effort that would take, how likely is that peace to last? For how long?

9. Reflecting on these bad things that could happen if you resolve your conflict, which ones are the most likely to happen? Least likely? Which ones would be the most difficult for you and those closest to you? The least?

10. Thinking of the worst thing that could happen if you resolved your conflict, if it happened, would it be devastating to you tangibly or psychologically or both? Could it also jeopardize—or ruin—your future and the future of those who matter to you the most? ***If so, would the potential damage be so great that if it happened, resolving this conflict would not be worth taking the risk, no matter how low the odds?***

Given that sometimes a single *cost* can outweigh any *benefit*, or any combination of benefits, or even all of them, do any of the costs of resolving your conflict do that?

For that matter, do all or any of the *benefits* that you also came up with of resolving your conflict outweigh the *costs*?

Decision Check-in #2

✓ If you were inclined toward resolving your conflict, has considering the costs of doing so changed your mind at all? If not, then your decision is most likely "Yes."

Note that a lot of people who decide "Yes–Resolve" after working through the questions of the benefits, costs, and future of "yes" find that that is all they need to reach their decision. They typically don't feel the need to answer the questions in the second triangle, namely, the benefits, costs, and future of "No–Don't Resolve."

✓ Even if you've made up your mind to resolve your conflict, my advice is that you take some time to consider the costs, benefits, and future of not resolving it. There is no harm in doing so and, if you've decided to resolve your conflict, going through the second triangle could confirm and even strengthen your decision.

✓ On the other hand, if you were leaning toward "No, don't resolve" has thinking about the costs of resolving your conflict strengthened this leaning? Has it even tipped the balance more toward "No?"

If your answer at this point is a pretty firm "No, don't resolve," or even if you're just leaning toward "No," it's important to consider both the positives and the negatives of this decision. In other words, now would be a good time to begin to consider the costs, benefits, and future of **_not_** resolving your conflict.

5.4 THE COSTS, BENEFITS AND FUTURE OF *NOT* RESOLVING YOUR CONFLICT: THE "NO, DON'T RESOLVE" TRIANGLE

As I mentioned in Section 5.2, choosing "No" can mean deciding not to resolve your conflict by not doing anything or by leaving the relationship, cutting all ties, and never seeing the person again.

Take a few moments to reflect on all the tangible and psychological benefits of resolving your conflict you came up with earlier in this chapter. These benefits would all be gone if you were to end your relationship. So, keep in mind that depending on how much they matter to you, losing them could add a lot to whatever other costs there are of saying goodbye.

5.4.1 QUESTIONS ABOUT THE IMMEDIATE COSTS OF *NOT* RESOLVING YOUR CONFLICT

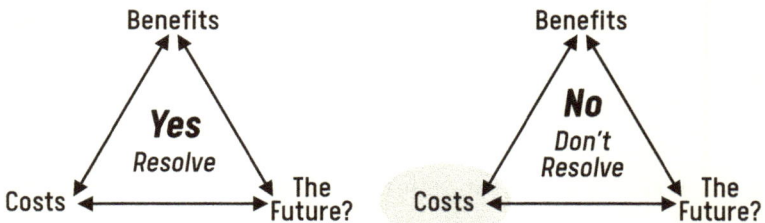

In the questions that follow, choosing "No" can mean deciding not to resolve the conflict by not saying or doing anything, or deciding not to resolve it (or to finally stop trying) by leaving the relationship, cutting all ties, and perhaps never seeing the person again. Not resolving a conflict and possibly ending a relationship, particularly a close and long-standing one, rarely happens without there being at least some tangible or psychological cost. Plainly speaking, while not resolving a conflict may have its benefits, it also almost always has its costs.

What Would the Likely Immediate Tangible Costs Be of Not Resolving Your Conflict?

The Likely Immediate Tangible Costs of Not Doing Anything

1. Are there any bad things with tangible costs that would likely happen right away if you don't do anything? If so, what would any of these cost you in terms of money, time, convenience, or health? How about for those who matter to you the most?
2. Are there any tangible things that you won't get or won't get back if you don't do anything? What tangible impact would that have on you and those closest to you?
3. Are there any tangible costs to your relationship that would likely increase right away if you don't do anything? What tangible impact would that have for you and those closest to you?
4. Is it likely that you'd be worse off tangibly right away or very soon if you don't do anything to resolve your conflict?

The Likely Immediate Tangible Costs of Ending Your Relationship

1. If you were to end your relationship, what bad things could happen that have tangible costs? For example:
    *   Could there be a financial cost to ending your relationship, such as the loss of a second income,

having to pay some form of compensation or
financial settlement, or having to pay legal or other
professional fees?

- Could there also be other costs such as lost
property, lost time, or inconvenience? Could it also
affect your health? What help would you no longer
have or be able to count on?
- Would this mean giving up some or all of what you
have already tangibly invested or built together?

2. Overall, would you be worse off right away if you
ended this relationship? If so, how much worse off?
For how long?

What Would the Likely Immediate <u>Psychological</u> Costs Be of <u>Not</u> Resolving Your Conflict?

The Likely Immediate <u>Psychological Costs</u> of Not Doing Anything

1. If you think you'd be tangibly worse off tangibly if you
didn't do anything, what psychological impact would this
have on you and those closest to you?
2. If you don't do anything, would the other person remain
unaware that they've done something wrong or that
something's bothering you?
3. How likely is it that the other person would mistakenly
see your silence as signaling to them that you're OK with
whatever it was they did?
4. If you don't do anything, is the conflict likely to go away
on its own?
5. What would be the psychological cost to you of not
saying anything about what's bothering you (e.g., would
you have to put your feelings of anger, frustration or hurt
on your emotional credit card)?

6.   Have you already not been doing anything about what the other person does for a while? As a result, is your emotional credit card nearing its limit?

7.   If you feel at least partly responsible for starting the conflict, and you don't at least say something, how badly would you feel about not admitting to your share of the responsibility or not apologizing for it?

8.   If you don't do anything, what relationship minuses and flashpoints would you have to continue to put up with? How big a strain would it be to for you to continue to put up with them? How about for those who matter to you the most?

9.   Would you have to change somehow to be able to continue to put up with these relationship minuses and flashpoints?

10.   Are there people you don't like who you'd have to stay friends with or make friends with if you did nothing to resolve this conflict? If so, how hard would that be?

11.   Would you have any regrets that you don't say anything, or that you don't at least try to resolve this conflict? Would anyone else close to you regret it as well?

12.   Is there anything about this decision that would go against your values or conscience?

13.   What is the worst thing that could happen right away if you don't do anything? What are the chances of this thing happening?

The Likely Immediate _Psychological Costs_ of Ending Your Relationship

1.   Apart from you and the other person, is there anyone who matters to you who would be upset if you ended your relationship? How much would that cost you emotionally? How long would it take to pass?

2.   If tangible costs are a consequence of ending your relationship, what would the psychological cost be of

dealing with those tangible losses for you and those closest to you? For example: What possessions would you miss? What creature comforts would you miss? What stresses or hardships would you or those closest to you have to endure?

3. Despite doing your best to cut your losses, if you had to give up at least some of what you've invested or built together in this relationship, how hard would this be psychologically on you? On those closest to you?

4. How much have you invested emotionally in this relationship? How hard would that be to let go of? Is what you've invested emotionally one of the things that is keeping you from ending this relationship?

5. If you ended your relationship how much would you miss the other person or the good aspects of your relationship? Which psychological benefits (e.g., fireworks) would you have to live without, at least for a while? How long? How difficult would this be?

6. If you ended your relationship would there be social consequences that are hard to take? For example, are there important relationships that could end or be damaged? How much conflict would this create? How much strain would this put on you and those who mean the most to you?

7. Could there be other social consequences that are hard to take like being rejected by certain people because you ended your relationship?

8. Could you lose the respect or admiration of certain people if you ended this relationship? If so, who, and how hard would that be on you?

9. Is there a relationship you have with someone else that you'd have to end if you ended this relationship? If so, what would be the impact on you and those closest to you?

10. Would there be things about this decision that you may regret? If so, what would they be and how difficult would

that be on you? Would anyone else close to you regret it as well?

11. How difficult would it be emotionally to end this relationship? Would this end to your relationship be difficult emotionally for those who matter to you the most? If so, how difficult?

12. How much do you already have on your plate? Do you have the strength right now to go through with it?

13. How much effort would it take for you to adapt to life without the other person? How about those who matter to you the most?

14. What impact would this decision have on those closest to you? How long would it take for them to get over it?

15. Is there anything about this decision that would go against your values or conscience?

5.4.2 QUESTIONS ABOUT THE POSSIBLE FUTURE COSTS OF *NOT* RESOLVING YOUR CONFLICT

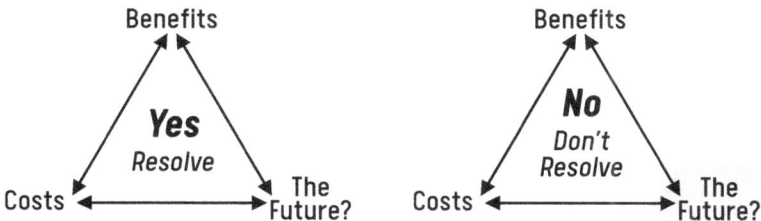

How Bad Could Things Get if You <u>Don't</u> Resolve Your Conflict?

Possible Future <u>Tangible</u> Costs

1. What bad things with tangible costs could happen long-term if you did not resolve your conflict? What

would be their tangible impact on you and those who
matter to you the most?

2. If there are tangible costs sooner or later to not resolving
    your conflict, how long would it take to, for example,
    make back the money you lost or get back on your feet
    financially, or simply recover from the loss? How confident
    are you that you could do so?

3. Are there privileges or perks that you would have to give
    up? If so, what are they and what could that mean to you
    and the people who matter to you the most?

Possible Future _Psychological Costs_

1. Turning now to possible future psychological costs if you
    don't do anything to resolve your conflict:

    - How long could you go on not doing anything?
    - If it doesn't go away on its own, could your conflict
      get worse? If so, how much worse? How likely is it
      to get worse?
    - If the other person did whatever it was that was a
      problem again and again, how long could you put
      up with it? What would be the emotional cost to
      you and those who mean the most to you?
    - How long do you think it would be before your
      positivity account hit zero or for your emotional
      credit card to "max out"?
    - Could things get so bad that not resolving your
      conflict now might lead to your relationship
      ending sooner or later anyway (or so strained that
      you end up wishing it would)? How likely is that?

2. Are there other unresolved conflicts that you have with the other person besides the one you're thinking of right now that are adding to the psychological costs to you of this relationship?
3. If you ended this relationship, how long and how much effort would it take to find and bring a new relationship to the same level of closeness that you once had? What are the chances of finding someone new?
4. Could there be some future opportunities lost, or doors closed, if you end this relationship?
5. Would or could any of these costs be permanent? Of those that are not, how long would they last? Which ones would last the longest time? Which ones the shortest? Could any costs outlive you and affect, for example, your children or other family members?
6. What is the worst thing that could happen if you end your relationship? What are the chances of it happening?
7. Thinking of the worst thing that could happen, if it happened, could it jeopardize—or even ruin—your future and the future of those who matter to you the most? *If so, would the potential damage be so great that ending your relationship is not worth taking the risk?*

Decision Check-in #3

✓ If you were inclined to resolve your conflict, it's likely that considering the costs of <u>not</u> resolving it has strengthened the inclination to resolve.
✓ If, on the other hand, you were leaning toward not resolving your conflict, did considering the costs of not doing so, make you pause and rethink this option?

5.4.3 QUESTIONS ABOUT THE IMMEDIATE BENEFITS OF
NOT RESOLVING YOUR CONFLICT

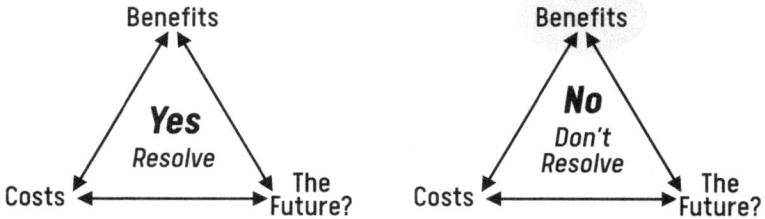

Benefits

Yes
Resolve

Costs The Future?

Benefits

No
Don't
Resolve

Costs The Future?

Although it can be hard to admit, there are sometimes benefits to not resolving a conflict—benefits that you could call the "silver lining." So, in these last two sets of questions, I'd like you to think about what good things could happen right away, and then what good things could happen in the future if you decide either not to do anything to resolve your conflict or decide to end your relationship.

Take a few moments to review all the costs you listed earlier of resolving your conflict. Whatever the costs there might be of resolving it, one of the potential benefits of ending your relationship is that you'll likely never have to worry about any of these costs again!

What Would the Likely Immediate <u>Tangible</u> Benefits—or Silver Lining—Be if You <u>Don't</u> Resolve Your Conflict

The Likely Immediate <u>Tangible</u> Benefits of Not Doing Anything

1. Is it possible that not resolving this conflict (or at least not yet) could have some tangible silver lining benefits right away (e.g., not costing you money or time or convenience)?
2. From the point of view of preserving the tangible assets and benefits of your relationship, could not doing anything be the best way of keeping your options open, at least for the time being?

The Immediate <u>Tangible Benefits</u> of Ending Your Relationship

1. Could there be any direct tangible benefits to ending your relationship (e.g., a financial settlement that comes to you)?

2. Are there any other things that could happen right away if you ended your relationship that would have tangible benefits for you and those closest to you? For example, what time and money would you now not have to spend? Which inconveniences would you now no longer have to bear?

Remember, ending your relationship could mean freeing up tangibles like money or time that you could then spend on someone–or something–else.

---

3. Could ending this relationship prevent any bad things from happening that, if they happened, would likely have a tangible impact on you and those who matter to you the most?

What Would the Likely Immediate <u>Psychological Benefits</u> Be if You <u>Don't</u> Resolve Your Conflict?

The Likely Immediate <u>Psychological Benefits</u> of Not Doing Anything

1. Would it be better emotionally for you to not do anything? For example, are you too emotionally drained or have too much on your plate to deal with this right now? Are there bad feelings that would be prevented or delayed by not doing anything, at least right away?

2. Is this the best time to even start trying to resolve this conflict? Would waiting for a more opportune time make more sense? In other words, can trying to resolve this conflict wait? And if so, how long?

The Likely Immediate _Psychological Benefits_ of Ending Your Relationship

1. If there are any tangible benefits of ending your relationship, could these be of some consolation to you—and those closest to you? In other words, could they help you cope with any of the psychological costs of ending it?
2. What psychological silver lining could there be for you and those closest to you if you ended this relationship? For example:
    - Is there anyone who matters to you who would be happy that you ended your relationship?
    - Would conflicts with those people who would be upset if you stayed in the relationship now not happen?
    - Would ending this relationship give you a chance to emotionally recover (e.g., from its flashpoints, conflicts, frustrations, and disappointments)? How long would that recovery take?
    - Would ending this relationship earn you approval, praise, admiration, or respect from important people in your life?
    - Would you be free of whatever hold or influence the other person had on you?
    - What flashpoints would you no longer have to put up with?
    - What effort would you no longer have to make?
    - What problems that the other person has would you be spared? That is, what problems, literally, would no longer be yours?

- How big a relief could that also be for those who matter to you the most?
- What things would you not have to do that you didn't like—or hated—doing?
- Would you be free to make new friends? If so, is there anyone you have in mind?
- Could you become closer to someone special? Restore or repair one or more important relationships?
- Would you no longer have to lie or deceive anyone about this relationship? How much a relief would that be?
- How much of a relief would it be to not have to spend the effort needed to resolve this conflict or to keep it resolved?

3. Would, emotionally speaking, this be all for the best; that is, the best thing for both of you and for all concerned?

5.4.4 QUESTIONS ABOUT THE POSSIBLE FUTURE BENEFITS OF *NOT* RESOLVING YOUR CONFLICT

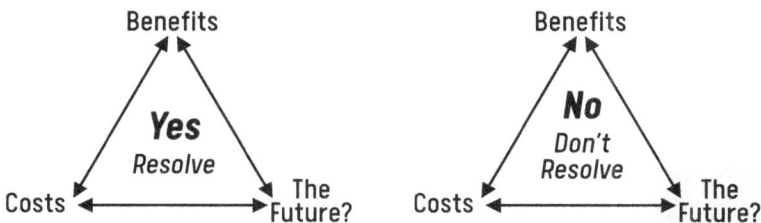

How Good Could the Future Be for You and Those Who Matter to You the Most if You Don't Resolve Your Conflict?

Possible Future <u>Tangible Benefits</u> of Not Doing Anything or of Ending Your Relationship

1. In addition to the good things that could happen right away, what good things and their benefits could happen over the long term (months or years from now)?
2. How confident are you of these good things and their benefits materializing sooner or later?
3. Would any of the benefits they bring be permanent? Of those that are not, how long would they last? Which ones would last the longest time? Which ones the shortest?

Possible Future <u>Psychological Benefits</u> of Not Doing Anything or of Ending Your Relationship

1. If there are any tangible benefits, what would be the psychological impact on you and those closest to you?
2. Of the immediate psychological silver lining benefits you see for you and those closest to you of you not doing anything or ending this relationship, what would be their long-term benefits?
3. Would, emotionally speaking, this be all for the best? That is, the best thing for both of you and for all concerned?
4. Could not resolving your conflict be a chance for you to make a fresh start? How confident are you that you could do that?
5. How confident are you that, if you wanted to, you could find someone new? Someone better matched? How long would that take? Or do you have someone already in mind?

In addition to any of the benefits of ending your relationship, you also avoid any of the bad things and risks there may have been of staying in it.

Note too that if you decide to end a relationship in which there would have been a high risk of something bad happening, then you might actually be preventing a catastrophe.

Given that a single benefit can outweigh any or all costs, do any of the benefits of not doing anything to resolve your conflict, or ending your relationship, have this effect?

Do any of the costs that you came up with outweigh some or all the benefits of not doing anything to resolve your conflict or ending your relationship?

Decision Check-in #4

If you were leaning towards "Yes-Resolve," did considering the questions on the possible silver lining and future benefits of not resolving your conflict change your mind at all?

If, on the other hand, you were leaning towards "No-Don't resolve," chances are that considering the plusses of not resolving your conflict helped you finalize your decision.

5.5 COMING TO YOUR DECISION

In a nutshell, the reasons to resolve a conflict boil down to you believing that, after taking everything into consideration, the benefits, costs, and future of "Yes, resolve" outweigh the benefits, costs, and future of "No, don't." Have you come to a decision?

Whether your decision is "Yes" or "No" remember that no one's perfect and no one makes perfect decisions all the time. Sometimes we say "Yes" when we should have said "No." Sometimes the reverse is true. Sometimes we should have said neither and waited... But it is my sincere hope that my decision-guiding triangles and their questions were helpful to you in reaching your decision, and that they will help you make good decisions in the future. I'm also hopeful, of course, that if you used them to take another look at a past decision, they helped you see what you might have done differently or helped confirm your original decision.

What if you haven't decided yet? What if you're not sure yet, one way or the other? It's perfectly OK to say, "I don't know." And it's OK to say, "I don't know, yet." Sometimes making important decisions is a very gradual process that takes a long time and cannot be rushed. If you haven't made up your mind yet, remember that:

- Whatever you do, as I mentioned earlier, never allow anyone to pressure you into making a decision that, for whatever reason, you are not yet ready to make. This having been said, if you do need more time and someone's waiting, keep them posted. Don't leave them in the dark.
- Sometimes you can't possibly decide yet because there are just too many unknowns, and only time will tell. In this case, often the best thing to do—as difficult as it can be—is to wait and see how things unfold.
- Sometimes you just need to take a break from actively thinking about it; that is, allow your answers to the hardest questions to bubble up in their own time.

- Bear in mind that sometimes you must also accept how you *really* feel about someone before you can make a decision. Accepting how you truly feel in your heart of hearts about someone—especially if you'd rather not admit it—can take a long time.
- Note also that, for a lot of people, the benefits of any really important decision must outweigh its costs by a wide margin before they can make that decision. A small difference that just tips the balance may not be enough. In this case too, only time will tell, and waiting to see how the cards fall might be the best thing to do.
- Another question to consider if you're not sure enough one way or the other is this: What would it take to make you sure enough? What conditions, if met, could make the difference?
- Is there anything you could do to make this happen? Is there something the other person could do? Is there something someone else could do to help?
- Would it help if you made the decision conditional? For example, saying "Yes, I'll try to resolve our conflict, if you _____." or "No, I won't try to resolve our conflict, unless you _____."
- Finally, it may also be a good idea to ask yourself what is holding you back from <u>acting</u> on your decision? As I mentioned earlier in this chapter, acting on a decision can be just as hard as coming to it and this can be one of the reasons behind not being able to make it.

**Just because a decision is the right one,
doesn't make it an easy one.**

A final word....

In the end, a lot of things can influence the outcome of any attempt you and the other person make to resolve a conflict, but at least two of them are essential: Motivation and communication—in other words, the will and the way. *If you have both, the resolution of your conflict is often not a question of "if," it's a question of "when."* Where there's a will (on both sides), there's a way. We now turn to the last chapter of this book, which focuses on the ins and outs of navigating resolution, the key to which is that second essential ingredient of successful conflict resolution, communication.

HOW TO NAVIGATE THE RESOLUTION
OF YOUR CONFLICT

What's Coming Up in this Chapter...

This chapter presents what I'm confident you'll find helpful in navigating each step of the conflict resolution process. To do this, I'll first provide you with some general guidelines and suggestions about how to communicate when in conflict.

Next, I'll walk you through each of the four steps of the conflict resolution process. If you don't remember these off the top of your head, they are: Offering an olive branch, unpacking your conflict, resolving any disagreements that arise from unpacking your conflict, and, reconciling and celebrating in some way. I'll also provide some advice around apologizing, how to deal with conflicts around differences in values, and relationship rearrangement. For each of these aspects of the conflict resolution process, I'll make suggestions and sometimes pose questions to help you decide what you do at each point. Speaking of decisions, and before moving on, I'd like to tell you about one more use for the cost-benefit-future triangle.

> Worksheets for this chapter are available from
> **www.theconflictresolvingnetwork.com**

6.1 ONE MORE IMPORTANT USE FOR THE
COST-BENEFIT-FUTURE TRIANGLE

The aim of the previous chapter was to help you decide whether to resolve your conflict using two cost-benefit-future triangles (one for "yes" and one for "no") as your guide. However, you can also use a single cost-benefit-future triangle to help you make all sorts of other decisions that come up in conflict which can make a big difference in how things unfold.

Imagining what the other person's cost-benefit-future triangles may be behind something they did can be really helpful for gaining insight and understanding of their perspective and what may have motivated them to do whatever it was that they did. *Just be watchful for making any assumptions that could turn out to be wrong.*

The Three Conflict-Preventing "Quickie Questions"

"An ounce of prevention is worth a pound of cure."

BENJAMIN FRANKLIN
(ONE OF THE FOUNDERS OF THE UNITED STATES OF
AMERICA, 1706–1790)

When in conflict, and especially when caught up in the moment, you typically face an immediate decision about what to say or do next and don't have time to carefully consider all your options. Sometimes you don't have to decide right there and then, but you still don't have enough time to consider your options in the sort of detail presented in Chapter 5. So, what do you do? One thing you can do is ask yourself the following three questions before deciding what to do:

1. **What good could this do?**
2. **What damage could this do?**
3. **Is it worth it?**

Just as every conflict unfolds one decision at a time, so too does its resolution. Asking yourself these three "quickie questions" also has the power to be **_conflict-preventing_**. They put the decision-making process of Chapter 5 in a nutshell. You can use them to weigh your options whenever you need to make a decision at any stage of any conflict and at any point in the conflict resolution process. For example:

- ✓ Do I speak out if something's bothering me (i.e., if something the other person said or did is a flashpoint for me)?
- ✓ Do I tell the other person what's bothering me when I'm asked: "Is anything the matter?"
- ✓ Do I drop hints about what's bothering me?
- ✓ Do I tell the other person why what they're doing is a flashpoint for me?
- ✓ Do I put it on my emotional credit card?
- ✓ Do I get even?
- ✓ Do I escalate?
- ✓ Do I de-escalate?
- ✓ Do I call a truce?
- ✓ Do I accept a truce?
- ✓ Do I disengage?
- ✓ Do I tell someone about what happened (e.g., close friend) and get their perspective?
- ✓ Do I offer the other person an olive branch?

✓ Do I accept the other person's olive branch?

✓ Do I "sweeten" my peace offering?

✓ Do I admit it's my fault?

✓ Do I apologize?

✓ Do I listen to the other person's apology?

✓ Do I accept the other person's apology?

✓ Do we talk about how we got into this conflict in the first place?

✓ Do I believe the other person?

✓ Do I give the other person the benefit of the doubt?

✓ Do I listen to my intuition?

✓ Do I compromise?

✓ Do I trust the other person?

✓ Do I forgive the other person?

✓ Do I give this relationship another chance?

✓ Do I come back?

✓ Do I say goodbye?

✓ Do I cut all ties and burn all bridges?

✓ Do I ghost the person?

✓ Do I suggest we try to be friends?

✓ If we can't be friends, do I suggest that we at least be on friendly terms?

✓ Do I decide what to do right now or do I give myself some time?

✓ Is this argument or conflict even worth having?

You may not always be able to think of the three quickie questions in the heat of the moment but when you can, and if you do, they can help a lot. After all, the best form of conflict resolution is stopping one from starting in the first place!

Every great relationship is the result of a thousand decisions.
The same is true of every bad one.

Can you think of situations in which using the quickie
questions might have been–or might still be–helpful to
you in making an important decision?

6.2 COMMUNICATING WHEN IN CONFLICT

"Between what is said and not meant,
and what is meant and not said,
most of love is lost."

KHALIL GIBRAN
(LEBANESE-AMERICAN WRITER, POET AND
VISUAL ARTIST, 1883-1931)

As I said earlier, the best place to start in conflict resolution is with clarity. To resolve conflicts you need to communicate honestly and clearly to one another. One of the most important things to be clear about—and to make clear to the other person—*is what you are feeling and why.* The other person may also want to do the same thing.

Clear communication is essential to getting to know one another better as time goes on. It is also the key to learning things about one another that may come in handy when faced with a conflict. This is because when in conflict, the less you know about one another, the more both of you will go by your imagination to fill in any gaps. This can be a big problem because your imagination can then carry you away, way off the mark—especially if trust between you hasn't had a chance to build or is low for whatever reason.

Simply put, without enough communication, too much is left to the imagination, which can be disastrous. ***Remember, communication without trust goes nowhere and trust without communication doesn't take you far enough.*** Indeed, it's hard to imagine a scenario in which you could ever over-communicate in a clear and open way in the resolution of a conflict.

Here are some points to consider when you're having a conversation with someone to resolve a conflict.

- First off, you're talking, and that's a good thing (the longer you don't talk about the conflict, the harder it'll be to start). As hard as communicating during a conflict is, with every little success you have, the easier these conversations get.
- Remember what I said in Chapter 3: When in conflict, emotions can "hijack" your thinking and leave you at a loss for words or cause you to choose words that you regret later. This is especially true when tempers flare!

Always remember that when feelings run high, not everyone says what they mean or means what they say. So, when you can, try to cut one another some slack.

Especially when your positivity account is overdrawn and your emotional credit card is maxed out, harsh words come to mind more quickly than kind ones.

- As much as emotions can get in the way, ***never ridicule, or put down the other person's feelings or the reasons they give you for feeling the way they do.*** It's tempting to do so, especially if you feel you're being attacked, unfairly accused, or think that the other person is over-reacting. You're much better off saying something like: "I get why you feel that way." than you are making fun of or trivializing the other person's feelings, or reasons for them.

- Always give each other the chance to tell one another *without being interrupted* what happened from their point of view. Even if you totally disagree with what the other person is saying, as hard as it may be for you, let them have their say.

- Also always give yourselves the chance to tell one another *—again without being interrupted—*how you feel about what the other person did (the relationship flashpoints exercise in Chapter 3 can help both of you with this). And remember, as also mentioned in Chapter 3, feelings can't go unexpressed for long—so they just build up. Interrupting one another blocks expression, which often triggers escalation.

It can be really hard to resist the temptation to interrupt one another. So, if you're both open to it, make a "No interrupting each other!" ground rule for these sorts of conversations. This can help, though at first it likely won't be easy for either of you to stick to this rule.

A lot of things in a relationship may have to start off as rules. But, if you both make an effort to stick to them, in time they become habits, which makes everything easier. *Habit, once established, eases effort.*

- Ideally, you both have a positive and open mind, and share a genuine desire to make things better. If this is not the case (being positive is sometimes not easy), it's important to *be aware of your frame of mind—that is, your mindset or stance—coming into your conversation.* For example:

- ○ Do you expect to be attacked or at least criticized during this conversation, regardless of what you say or do? As a result, are you in a defensive or "bunker mentality" frame of mind?
- ○ Along the same line, do you feel like you're going into some kind of battle with the other person? Does it seem that all they want to do is fight and you'll have to fight back?
- ○ Maybe you don't want a fight at all, but you're assuming that no matter how your conversation starts, it'll end in one.
- ○ Are you angry? Does part of you want revenge for what the other person did? Are you itching for a fight, or do you just want to clear the air?
- ○ Are you feeling vulnerable? Apprehensive? If you are, bear in mind that this can make you feel defensive as well.
- ○ Are you feeling exasperated? Are you saying to yourself something like: "I told you a thousand times not to do that!" or "Here we go again!"? Or maybe you're asking yourself, *"Now* what did I do!?" or "What the _____ do you want from me?"
- ○ Are you coming into the conversation weighed down by a sense of hopelessness or dread? Do you expect your conversation to go nowhere except in circles?

If you answered "yes" to any of these, it's entirely possible that your feelings and stance are justified. After all, if you know the other person well enough and if this is how previous attempts to resolve your conflicts have gone, you may well be right. You may also be wrong, but the suggestion I want to make here is that ***whatever your frame of mind coming into the conversation is, try not to think of whatever you're expecting to happen as a foregone conclusion.***

Why? If you do, your expectation can come true. How? Your attitude coming into the conversation is likely hard to hide. If the other person picks up on it, they will likely react in ways that match your mood. Once this starts to happen, the pattern you expect to unfold could unfold, in which case your expectation becomes a self-fulfilling prediction. Remember, expectation can easily become reality. *However, also remember that all it takes is just one instance of breaking a pattern to, potentially, begin its slow but steady reversal.*

Remember inner escalation mentioned in Chapter 3?
Be aware that, depending on your frame of mind,
you can start imagining all kinds of bad outcomes
of your conversation and get very worked up before
either of you have even said a word.

- *Be selective about what you focus on in what you say.*
  Remember that there's only so much you can say at a time and only so much the other person can take in at one time.
- *Prioritize.* If you've got more than one conflict going on with someone, don't try to resolve them all at once. Either pick the one that matters the most to you or, if none of them are all that important, ask yourself—using the three quickie questions—whether the conflict you could get into is even worth having. Always think twice before spending whatever goodwill or positivity you have with someone on an argument or fight that could cost you your relationship.
- *Listen.* As critical as talking is to conflict resolution, talking without listening doesn't get you very far either. Listening is critical to conflict resolution for a lot of reasons. For example:

- ○ Listening shows respect. It also shows that whatever it is the other person is trying to get across to you matters enough to give it your full attention.
- ○ When you've been listening, you're able to speak to what the other person has been saying. Moreover, you can occasionally repeat in your own words (or sum up) what the other person has been saying to show that you've been listening, and as a way of checking to make sure you've got what they've been saying right.
- ○ Being listened to is inherently de-escalating. In contrast, when people don't feel listened to, they'll often raise their voice, which is one of the first steps on the road to escalation.

You know you're *not* really listening when all you're thinking about while the other person is talking is what you're going to say when they're done.

- ○ Remember too that simply listening and not saying anything is often more welcomed and helpful than jumping in with advice. And if you want to offer advice, always ask the other person if they want to hear it first.
- ○ In the same vein, remember that empathy can be more wanted and needed than advice.

- Listening to yourself is important too. When tensions are high, how you say something can be as important as what you say.
- When emotions are running high in conflict conversations, the smallest gesture can speak volumes.

- Watch your use of words like "everybody," "nobody," "never," "everything" and "always." The problem with saying "you never…" or "you always…" is that all it takes for the other person is to come up with the one time that was the exception to throw you off completely. It's much better to use words like "sometimes," "often," "a lot of the time," "rarely," "hardly ever," etc.

- Although this is obvious, it's worth remembering that saying things like "Who cares?" or "I don't care!" or "So what?" are all going to be flashpoints for the other person, and an almost surefire recipe for escalation. Anyone for whom something matters will feel that you're disrespecting them when you use such words, and they'll likely want to retaliate.

- Speaking of words to avoid, using the word "you" a lot can sound like you think you have the other person all figured out and that you know exactly what they're thinking and feeling. They will likely resent this, and it can simply be denied each time you say something that sounds that way.

- Using "you" a lot can also sound like you're blaming the other person. When you start saying things like: "You think of no one but yourself!" "You have no idea how I feel!" or "Your job is more important to you than your family!"—once again—the other person can simply deny it. This, of course, leads to the conversation going round in circles.

- Try to stick to speaking for yourself only. Speaking for yourself means using so-called "I-statements" (e.g., I think, I feel, I have, I see, I am) as often as you can, as opposed to using "you." It's much harder for the other person to deny what you say you're thinking or feeling than it is for them to deny whatever you claim *they're* thinking or feeling.

- Try to make sure that anything you say that needs to be purely objective (i.e., factually correct) is beyond a shadow of a doubt (e.g., dates, times, places, events). Disagreement over facts that can be doubted or denied can easily send your conversation into a tailspin.
- Say something to acknowledge whenever the two of you do agree on something. It's also worth acknowledging when the other person makes a good point by saying something like: "You're right about that." "That's a good point." "I'll grant you that." "I get what you're saying." "Well, when you put it that way...."
- If and when the other person admits to something that you were right about all along, try not to gloat or rub it in. ***Try to be gracious and always let the other person save face.***
- In some situations, with some people, you might not feel close enough to tell them __*why*__ what they did is a flashpoint for you. Maybe you're embarrassed that you ***have such*** a flashpoint and don't want to talk about what happened to you that made it one. You might expect that, even if you did tell the other person, you'd get into an argument over whether it should be a flashpoint in the first place. You might also feel that they'd likely make fun of you or put you down for having such a flashpoint. Consider this: Despite it all, sometimes, taking this risk can open up communication between the two of you and make all the difference. This is another decision that the three quickie questions can help you make (i.e., What good could this do? What damage could this do? Is it worth it?).
- Especially if the stakes are high, you can be justifiably anxious about what the other person may think, feel, say, or do during your conversation. ***Sometimes you have to muster the courage to tell the other person what you think they need to hear and ask them the questions that you need answers to.***

- Conversations when in conflict can be difficult for both of you. It can be hard to say what you need to say to the other person, and it may be hard to listen to what the other person has to say. ***Remember that it's perfectly OK to admit to the other person how hard having this conversation is for you. You can say something like: "This is really hard for me to say…" or "I don't know exactly how to put this…" or "I want the best for us, and I hope you don't take this the wrong way…"***

As I noted in Chapter 5, sometimes, speaking out and enduring a few minutes of awkwardness and discomfort can save you years of unhappiness, conflict, and grief!

- Ideally, you'll reach a point in the conversation when the uphill climb is over, the tension has broken, and resolution and reconciliation doesn't seem far away. ***It is a very good sign when that happens!***

6.3 WORKING THROUGH THE FOUR STEPS OF THE CONFLICT RESOLUTION PROCESS—STEP ONE: OFFERING AN OLIVE BRANCH

Now that we've covered some key guidelines and suggestions about how to communicate when in conflict, it's now time to turn to the four steps of the conflict resolution process.

Your first move can take many forms, but it typically involves offering the other person some token of goodwill or a peace offering (i.e., an olive branch). The olive branch offering can come after a period of disengagement, or it can be offered spontaneously in the middle of a conflict such as when one of you decides to de-escalate and sends a signal that says: "Let's stop this escalation right now before it goes too far!"

Speaking of signals, if the two of you have been disengaged for a while, sometimes neither of you wants to say something outright like "Do you want to talk?" So instead, consider coming up with a signal (e.g., a phrase like "Would you like a cup of tea?") that tells the other person you want to reconnect.

As I mentioned in Chapter 2, your olive branch may not get accepted at first, in which case you may need to "sweeten" it. If this happens, there could be some back-and-forth between the two of you (you may remember from Chapter 2 that I call this the olive branch dance). Typically, sooner or later, the other person will either accept your olive branch, or say "I'll think about it...," or they might reject it outright (in which case the two of you disengage again—perhaps for the last time, perhaps not).

If You're the One Offering an Olive Branch

- Offering an olive branch is taking a risk; so, it takes courage, confidence, and sometimes faith in yourself and the other person to do it. So, before you offer your olive branch, be absolutely sure you want to. If you're at all ambivalent, and if the three quickie questions don't clarify your decision, consider re-reading Chapter 5 to help you decide whether or not to make this all-important first move. It can mean a lot to the other person that you do want to resolve your conflict.

Is there such a thing as offering the olive branch too soon? Yes. This can happen if you haven't taken the time to fully think through your decision. Remember if you're not 100% sure you want to resolve the conflict, a peace offering that comes across as half-hearted is worse than no offering.

- Also know **_why_** you want to resolve your conflict. For example, during disengagement, did your flashpoint feelings fade and did you start to miss the other person? Did you decide that your relationship has enough plusses to make trying to resolve this conflict worth the effort (and worth taking the chance)? Is it conflict fatigue that's prompting you?
- Sometimes, all you need to get the ball rolling is to reach out with something like a text that reads: "Hi." Sometimes you need to say or do a lot more than that.
- How you reach out is up to you: It could be a text, an email, an ecard, a phone call, a present or a bouquet of flowers, all depending on your relationship.
- Remember that the way in which your olive branch is offered can be as important as—if not more important than—the olive branch itself!
- What's included in your olive branch offering is up to you, but whatever it is, it should fit the seriousness of the conflict (and what you've done to upset the other person), as well as how close the two of you are, how well you know each other, etc.
- In addition to simply being an invitation to re-engage, your peace offering should include an acknowledgment of the other person's feelings. It can also come with an admission of whatever your responsibility or fault is for what happened—whether it's total or partial—as well as an apology for whatever you did or didn't do. It could also include an offer to make amends, or the suggestion of a compromise.
- When you're sure you want to offer an olive branch, you might consider asking a someone like a trusted mutual friend to be a diplomatic go-between. This person could also help you further clarify your thoughts and feelings, choose what your olive branch offering might

be, and even smooth any ruffled feathers in advance of
your offer.

- You might also get your friend to help you put together
  what you want to say and, if need be, rehearse it.

- Never take away from the value of your offer by
  trivializing how the other person feels with an invitation
  that goes something like: "Are you over your tantrum
  now?" or "Are you ready to stop acting like a big baby?"
  It may be tempting, and not far from the truth, but it's a
  bad idea.

- Remember to give the other person the time they need to
  think about your offer. If you seem impatient, it might look
  like you're pressuring them. Even if it's subtle, it can be
  seen as pushiness or pestering, which is likely to backfire.

- As I mentioned earlier, your olive branch may get a
  lukewarm response or be ignored or rejected at first. This
  could be because of the way you offered it, what you
  offered, or a combination of both. If it's a rejection, this
  might be a signal for you to sweeten the offer. It may also
  be that the other person is just not interested in going any
  further with your relationship.

If You're the One Being Offered an Olive Branch

- Although the other person may have decided to reach out
  to you, you may not have come to the same decision yet.
  Take your time. If you're unsure or ambivalent, and if the
  three quickie questions don't work, consider re-reading
  Chapter 5 to help you decide whether to accept the other
  person's olive branch.

- Remember that there is such a thing as accepting an olive
  branch too soon if you're not fully ready. You are under
  no obligation to accept it right away.

- If the olive branch comes as a complete surprise and you're not quite sure you're ready to receive it, then tell the other person that you need some time to think about it.
- Even if you're open to accepting the olive branch, you might not feel there's enough in it given what the other person did. Just remember that if you're still angry, you may be tempted to repeatedly turn it down. Be careful not to do this too many times, as it may backfire.

Advice for the Both of You

- Although it's tempting to do this, try not to make the time you both spend in disengagement a "battle of wills" to see who "blinks" first. This happens when, out of sheer stubbornness, one or both of you refuse to make the first move.

Both of you wanting to reconnect but refusing to do so out of bullheadedness is like having a contest to see who can stay miserable the longest. Furthermore, if this contest goes on long enough, it can turn into relationship limbo. As I mentioned in Chapter 2, this can happen when two people refuse to speak to one another for months or even years, thereby closing the door on what might have been a great relationship.

6.3.1 APOLOGIZING

Sometimes apologizing is part of the olive branch offering and sometimes it comes later. In either case, there is no doubt that the words "I am sorry" have ended countless conflicts over the millennia and prevented countless more. These simple words are perhaps the most powerful and pivotal in all of conflict resolution.

In English, "I'm sorry" comes from the Old English word "sarig" meaning "distressed and full of sorrow." In other words, to say "I'm sorry" is to say, "I am distressed and full of sorrow for what I did," or more simply, "I am suffering because I made you suffer."

Everything I suggested to you about offering an olive branch applies to offering your apology. Except for this one more thing: ***How much someone really cares about you, how much they really care about your well-being and your relationship, how sincere they are, and how truly sorry and remorseful they are, is shown by how they apologize to you.*** There are few things worse for any kind of relationship and more damaging to it than an insincere apology. Insincere apologies look and sound flippant or mechanical, feel half-hearted, and give the impression that the other person has taken for granted that you'll accept their apology no matter what. Plainly put, an insincere apology adds insult to injury.

Making a genuine and sincere apology, like offering an olive branch, takes both humility and courage. You can feel a mix of different feelings like regret and remorse, along with possibly shame and guilt; and you can also feel vulnerable and nervous. You may even feel a bit defensive about having to admit to what it is you're apologizing for. In fact, it's such a complicated mix of emotions that when we're truly sorry for something we did, all we can usually say is something like "I feel really bad..." or "I feel awful."

If You're the One Offering an Apology

- As with offering an olive branch, be completely sure that you are ready to offer an apology.

- Apologize for what is your fault or, at least, what is your part of the fault for what happened. Don't apologize for something you didn't do just to end the conflict. Doing this might end the conflict (at least for a while), but it won't resolve it.
- Bearing in mind the seriousness of what it is you did, ask yourself: What do I say in my apology, given the impact of what I did had, tangibly and psychologically, on the other person? What do I owe this person? Is an apology enough? If not, what else can I offer the other person? What can I do to make things right?
- Be clear in your own mind about what it is you are apologizing for. Whatever it is, you should be able to say something about each of the four essentials; that is, admit to what it was you did that caused the other person's loss, what you intended, which relationship rule or rules you broke, and what your share is of the responsibility for what happened.
- After apologizing for what you know you needed to apologize for, ask if there is anything else you should apologize for. Sometimes there is, and you don't realize it.
- Be sure to also apologize for whatever you said or did during escalation too. In fact, both of you are likely to have some apologizing to do in this regard.
- When you offer an apology don't assume that it will be automatically accepted, or that an apology alone is going to make up for what you did. Always remember too that the other person does not have to accept your apology right away or, for that matter, ever.
- The other person may also have conditions they expect you to meet for your apology to be accepted.
- Not only does the other person not have to accept your apology—they don't even have to hear it if they don't want to. They can, if they wish, walk away, or tell you

not to bother even before you get a word (of apology) in edgewise.

- Even if your apology is accepted, if what you did has seriously set back your relationship, it may take a long time for things to get back to normal. It may also take some time for the other person to completely forgive you, or fully get over the emotional cost of what you did. *A clean slate with someone is not always an absolutely spotless slate.*

- If the conflict was all your fault, admit it and don't backpedal or try to come up with excuses.

- It's OK to explain yourself or provide a reason for what you did, but don't try and pass off your explanation as an excuse.

- If alcohol or some other substance influenced what you did, don't use your inebriation as an excuse. It may explain your lapse in judgment but does not excuse it. You were after all, the one who got yourself inebriated. Claiming "It was the liquor doing the talking" is not a defense. Do not try to blame what it was that intoxicated you for your intoxication and your behavior. Think of it this way: Alcohol doesn't get you drunk... you do.

- During your apology never bring up a flaw in the other person. People sometimes do this when feeling a bit defensive just so they can feel at least a little bit "right" about something. This just dilutes your apology, and it can make you sound petty. Furthermore, it can be seen as just an attempt to divert attention from what you did.

- Don't overdo saying self-punishing things like: "I don't know what's wrong with me—I can't believe I was so selfish!" "I'm such an idiot!" "I don't deserve you!" and so forth. Such statements may well be true at least to some extent, or feel to you that they are, but overdoing it can sound like you're fishing for sympathy.

- Don't say things that side-step your responsibility for what happened; for example, don't say: "I'm sorry if you feel that way." or "I regret that it happened." or "I'm sorry but you _____." Say instead—plainly and simply—"I'm sorry that _____ (e.g., I let you down)." This is a far more authentic, honest, and direct admission of, and apology for, what you did.
- For a lot of people, an apology sent by text for something serious isn't worth the pixels it's written in.
- Keep your apology straightforward and consider structuring it to reflect each of the four essentials.
    1. Admit what it was you did that caused the other person's ***loss***—whether tangible, psychological or both. That is, say something that shows you're admitting what you did and acknowledging the impact of what you did to the other person. You can say something like: "You have every right and reason to be angry at me." Saying how you feel about what you did is important too. For example:
        - "I owe you an apology. I'm sorry for what I said. I know it hurt you and I feel really bad about what I did."

    2. State what you ***intended***. For example:
        - "It was supposed to be a joke—but I realize that what I said was offensive."

    3. Acknowledge what relationship rule or rules you ***violated*** (whether you knew it or not). For example:
        - "I realize that what I said crossed the line. I should have known better."
        - "I know what I did was wrong. I shouldn't have...."

4. Acknowledge the degree of your ***responsibility*** for what happened. For example:

   ○ "I take full responsibility for my lapse in judgment."

- In addition to saying something about each of the four essentials, you should also:

   a. Promise that it won't happen again and what you're going to do to make sure it never does. For example:

      ○ "I deeply respect you and never want to offend you again. You have my word that I am going to be more mindful and considerate from now on. I promise you I will do my best to never let this sort of thing happen again."

   b. Offer to make amends. For example:

      ○ "What can I do to make it up to you?"
      ○ "Please allow me to make it up to you."

   c. If you can't make amends, then at least take responsibility.

   d. If you think you should, then ask to be forgiven. I discuss forgiveness in Section 6.6 which also covers the fourth and final step of the conflict resolution process.

- Whatever it is the person you're apologizing to wants to say, even if it's to vent—let them—listen to every word without saying a word. Whatever unflattering things the other person may have to say about you may just be part of your comeuppance, and they need to get it off their chest. Even if some things they say aren't entirely fair, now is not the time to argue.

- Speaking of comeuppance, there may be more in store. If you feel you deserve what could be coming, be willing to take it, and say so.
- Once you are ready to apologize, the sooner you do it, the better. If your apology is late in coming, then you should at least explain why it took you as long as it did to get around to apologizing.
- If at first you denied what you did but ended up having to admit or confess to it in the end, then you must apologize not only for whatever you had to admit to, but also for having lied.
- Be careful when using words like "yeah, sure," "anyway..." or "whatever..." Said in the wrong tone, they can sound disrespectful.
- Don't minimize the other person's loss in your apology. For example, don't refer to what happened as "a misunderstanding" if there was more to it than that (e.g., you're aware of what you did and why).
- If you owe the other person a really big apology, consider practicing your delivery with a friend.
- Saying sorry is as much about the future as it is about the past: Whether you state it or not, implicit in saying "I'm sorry" is promising that it won't happen again. This having been said, although making promises about how you'll change is important, don't over promise. Don't promise to try to change everything that you'd like to change about yourself all at once. Remember, change takes effort and willpower; trying to change too much too soon takes a lot of willpower which is likely to run out at some point. It is much better to under-promise and over-deliver than the other way around.

If You're the One Being Apologized to

- Remember, when you have been wronged you are, at the very least, owed an apology.
- Never accept an apology that you feel is not 100% genuine or until you are 100% ready to accept it. Most likely your intuition is a good judge of the sincerity of what you see and hear.
- Unless the other person springs their apology on you and it comes as a complete surprise, be sure that you're ready to hear it. If you're not sure yet, then thank the other person for their offer and tell them you're not ready yet.
- If you've decided that you're open to hearing the apology, and if there's some time before you have that conversation, consider the following:
  - When and where would be the ideal time and place for *you* to meet or chat? For example, when and where would there be no distractions for you? If it's possible, pick both the time and the place.
  - Also consider, is there anyone besides you who the other person should apologize to? If so, should the other person apologize separately or in front of the others who were affected too?
  - What is it you'd like to hear the other person say? What would be the minimum for you to accept their apology?
  - Is there anything you would like to know or have clarified? What questions do you want answers to?
  - Be honest with yourself: What in your heart of hearts would you like the outcome to be?

- As noted earlier, the apology should at least touch on all four essentials.

- There is always a chance that you'll be disappointed with the apology you get. If this has happened before with this person, consider what the consequences will be; that is to say, what you will do if their apology falls short.

- Reflect on your frame of mind. How are you feeling? Are you still a little angry? Hurt? Distrustful? If you're ready to talk, it's likely these feelings have faded enough. If they haven't entirely, be aware that whatever feelings you have may come out in some way or another and even in full force, depending on what the other person says or does during their apology.

- If you're still angry or hurt, you may want to get a lot of things off your chest. This could mean saying a lot of unflattering things to the other person, berating or scolding them, lecturing them, and even ranting about what they did. Just be careful not to take it too far.

- When someone knows they're in trouble for what they did, they could be sorrier for what's likely to happen to them than they are for what they actually did. *There is a big difference between being sorry out of dread or fear and being sorry out of genuine remorsefulness and caring for the other person and the relationship you have.*

- Watch your use of phrases like "That's OK..." or "It's alright..." They can be taken the wrong way. Take for example, a statement like "What you did to me was really hurtful, but I know you were pretty confused at the time so it's OK." It isn't clear if you mean that you're OK and have recovered from whatever the other person did, or that it's OK for the other person to do those things to you, or that you mean you forgive them. So, instead, you could say something like: "What you did to me was really hurtful, but I know you were pretty confused at the time. I accept your apology and I forgive you."

- You can accept an apology while not having completely forgiven—or forgotten—what the other person did. *Accepting an apology does not require forgiveness or amnesia.*
- *Never say "all is forgiven" if all is not forgiven.*
- Never make excuses for what the other person did or suggest excuses for them. You can certainly be understanding of why the other person did what they did and tell them so, but don't let your understanding be interpreted as excusing, justifying, or permitting them.
- Don't help the other person by giving them the words to apologize with or deliver the apology that you'd like to hear. *In other words, don't do the work for them—let them earn your acceptance of their apology.*
- It's good to be positive, upbeat, and even excited at the prospect of reconciling, but along the same line as the previous point, being too eager to reconcile can make it seem a little too easy for the other person. Again, let them earn your acceptance of their apology.
- Generally, apologies are hard to fully accept when:
  - It isn't the first time the other person has done whatever it is they are apologizing for.
  - The other person apologizes only because they think it will be advantageous to them to stay on your good side.
  - You have to ask (or demand) that the other person apologize.
  - You must extract a confession from them before they apologize.

- Remember that no matter how sincere the other person's apology, there must be a change!

> *"Trust only movement."*
>
> **ALFRED ADLER**
> (**AUSTRIAN MEDICAL DOCTOR AND**
> **PSYCHOTHERAPIST** 1870–1937)

- Pay greater attention to what the other person does than what they say they'll do, no matter how beautiful what they say sounds. Simply put, go more by what the other person does than what they say they'll do. As the old saying goes: Actions speak louder than words (another way of putting this is that actions often speak more truthfully than words).
- Make it clear to the other person if you've accepted their apology. Saying something as simple and straightforward as "I accept your apology" or "Apology accepted" will do and could be music to the other person's ears.
- If you don't think you can actually stay friends, be honest and say so; although, if you can't be friends, then perhaps you can agree to at least be on friendly terms.

Whether You Are the One Apologizing or Are Receiving the Apology

- Apologies typically start off as one-way conversations, but they often and very quickly become two-way conversations.
- A genuine and sincere apology offered and accepted can bring closure for both of you and allow you to move on.
- Sometimes a genuine and sincere apology by itself can resolve your conflict. Sometimes it's all that anybody wants; and sometimes, it's all anybody needs. How's that? If it took a certain amount of insight for the other person

to apologize to you, then by apologizing, they've shown there's likely no need for much more—or anymore—unpacking of what happened.

- Simply put, you both know and agree on what went wrong, what to do about it, and you're both committed to making sure it never happens again. So, if that is the case, you then go right on to Step Four, Reconciliation and Celebration.

6.4 STEP TWO: CONFLICT UNPACKING

The goal of this step is to sort out—that is, unpack—what happened, figure out what went wrong, and solve whatever the problem was together so that, ideally, you never have this particular conflict again. As I mentioned in Chapter 2, successful problem unpacking and problem solving can strengthen your relationship and change its trajectory; that is to say, it can change where and how far your relationship might go in the future. Although a lot of the time conflicts are resolved in Step Two, there are some challenges to be aware of:

- Where your positivity accounts stand with one another is always important, and it can be especially important at this step in the conflict resolution process. This is because during unpacking as you're thinking about what started your conflict in the first place, you can also be reminded of some of the bad things about the other person and your relationship—along with some flashpoint moments that you may have forgotten about (or wish you'd forgotten about).

- When unpacking it can be tempting to gloss over details of what happened between you. This is often out of not wanting to put a damper on the moment and possibly trigger another conflict. It can also be because, in the joy of the prospect of reconciling, whatever things you were both glossing over truly don't matter that much anymore.

- Whatever the reason, it may be wise to gloss over or even skip certain details (i.e., pick your battles), but it could be helpful to talk about things sooner or later—perhaps at a time at which you're both comfortable enough to open up with each other about what happened. In connection to this, by the way, most people only go as far as they need to (or at least as far as both are comfortable going) when unpacking.
- Sometimes people simply delay unpacking until they've rebuilt sufficient positivity back into their relationship, which can be a wise thing to do.
- Sometimes, as well, when there are several aspects to the unpacking and problem-solving of the conflict, it can take a while and can take more than one conversation.
- As I mentioned earlier in this chapter, listening is a top skill in conflict resolution, and it comes into play in spades during problem unpacking and problem solving.

6.4.1 UNPACKING WITH THE FOUR ESSENTIALS

One way to unpack your conflict is to use the four essentials. As you'll recall, all four essentials of conflict—loss, intent, violation, and responsibility—must be present for there to be conflict, and so *if any one of them is missing—for whatever reason—there is either less potential for conflict or no conflict at all*.

Always ask yourself what might be going on in the other person's mind with respect to their perception of loss, intent, violation, and responsibility. You may not be as far apart as you think!

As I pointed out in Chapter 1, all four essentials depend on interpretation and how you see each one. To be specific: How you see what's been lost by one or both of you (and the extent of this loss); what you intended or think the other person intended; what violation occurred and how serious that violation is; and, who you see as being responsible (and to what extent). *Sometimes the perception of loss, intent, violation, or responsibility is based entirely, or at least to some degree, on a misunderstanding, a mistaken assumption, an unjustified expectation, or on a fact that one or both of you got wrong.*

What this means is that if both of you are willing to re-examine the basis of your conclusions about one another's loss, intent, violation, and responsibility, it might be possible to "knock out," nullify, or at least put in doubt one of these essentials of conflict. In so doing you could nip your conflict in the bud, stop it cold, or at least de-escalate it a notch or two! *The idea in unpacking is to ask yourself—or one another—questions that could help you both re-think each other's loss, intent, violation, and responsibility.*

Although differences in perception are a common source of disagreement, this also means that there is often some room for interpretation, reinterpretation, or re-thinking around each of the four essentials. So, while on the one hand, interpretation can—and often does—pose a challenge; on the other hand, it's the room for interpretation inherent in a lot of situations that can give you both the flexibility and room to maneuver you need to resolve your conflict.

Don't forget about what you're both doing right. Be mindful of the fact that to have reached this step, you both must have done—and are doing—a lot of things right.

Questions for Re-thinking Loss

- Is it possible that one or both of you didn't hear or see clearly what the other person said or did? Is it possible that one or both of you misunderstood what the other person was trying to say or what they were doing?
- Could what either of you said or did have been said or done differently so as to be less of a loss for the other person (e.g., used words that were less harsh), but didn't—or don't—know how? If so, could you or the other person have said something right there and then? Could that have helped? If either of you said something now, could that still help the situation?

If you're ever really surprised, taken aback, or shocked by something the other person says or does–especially if it's something completely out of character for them–ask them to clarify what or why it is they said or did as soon as you can.

If you're not sure why, clarify!

And even if for whatever reason, you don't want to or can't ask right away (e.g., you're lost for words, you don't want to risk starting an argument, there are other people around) do it sooner than later.

You can say something very neutral but direct like: "What was that you said?" or, more softly, you could say: "The other day you said something that's not sitting quite right with me–and I just need to double-check with you...."

If ever in doubt, check it out!

*Of course, you could be right in your original take on what the person said or did... but what if you're not? **A misunderstanding (and the feelings that go with it) can be carried around for years before it finally–if ever–gets cleared up.***

Can a single misunderstanding put a long-lasting damper on a relationship? Yes. Can a structural conflict grow out of a single misunderstanding? Yes... and it can set in motion a slow but sure downward spiral in any relationship.

- Is it possible that one or both of you took what the other person did the wrong way? Is it possible that you or the other person read too much into it? Is it possible that one or both of you are taking it too hard or too seriously?

- Is it possible that the other person didn't know that what they did was a loss for you (psychologically or tangibly)? If not, can you tell them why it was or still is? Would that help the situation? What about the other way round? Is it possible that you didn't know that what you did would be a loss for the other person?

- Was this a one-off conflict situation? That is, was it a transitory conflict and not likely due to any deeper problem between the two of you?

- If there was escalation, did you both get carried away? If so, was what happened during escalation worse than what started it?

- Could one of you have called a truce? Should one of you have? Would that have helped the situation? Could you still call a truce? Would that help?

- Was—or is—there anything that was magnifying the loss for you? For the other person? For example, having a bad day, being stressed out, feeling on edge, feeling drained or depleted, feeling fed up and exasperated because of a history of conflict with the other person that goes back a long way, etc. Could any of these things have made the loss for you or the other person (tangible or psychological) seem greater than it may actually be?

- In the grand scheme of things, is this really as big a loss as it feels?
- How much could this loss (psychological, tangible or both) matter to you:
  - A month from now?
  - A year from now?
  - Five years from now?
  - Ten years from now?

- If there was tangible loss, how could the other person make things right? How could you make things right?
- As for your psychological loss, what would it take for the other person to make it up to you? Or for you to make it up to the other person?
- Upon reflection, could your loss be self-inflicted to some degree? Could it be at least partly based on a faulty expectation on your part? Self-inflicted doesn't mean deserved, but if it is self-inflicted to some extent, it could likely have been prevented. Remember, in Chapter 1 I said that not getting what you want is not the same thing as losing what you already have. Dashed hopes (e.g., unrequited love) and unfulfilled expectations, even if they are unfounded, often feel like a loss and lay at the core of many conflicts. How about the other person? Could their loss be self-inflicted?
- Is the flashpoint that the other person triggered in you completely understandable in this situation? If it is, that's one thing; but if it's not, then is it possible that you overreacted? Is it possible that this flashpoint is out of place in this situation? If it is, then is it fair to put the

responsibility of an out-of-place flashpoint on the other person and make it their problem to deal with? If it's not fair, then could, or should, you consider taking steps to "fix" this flashpoint in you? Could these questions also be put to the other person?

Questions for Re-thinking Intent

- How do you know that what the other person did was deliberate? Or premeditated? Could it be that what they did was done on impulse or that they were just not thinking? Could they have been preoccupied with something else?
- If it's something you did, what was your intent?
- If it was something you or the other person said, did you or the other person really mean it? Remember, being in the grip of a conflict can make people say and do things that they don't mean.
- If the other person meant what they said, what was their intent? Is it possible that, at least from their perspective, there was a perfectly reasonable explanation for what they did? For example, is it possible that they sincerely wanted to help and not hurt you?
- If they were sincere and meant well, did they know that what they said (or how they said it), or what they did, might embarrass you, hurt you, or anger you? If they didn't, should they have known? How could they have known?
- Is it possible that you incorrectly assumed what the other person would feel and how they would react?
- Is it possible that the other person has more on their plate than you realize? For example, are there things going on in their life that are draining their willpower, adding tensions to their life from many directions, and taxing

their tangible and psychological resources to the limit? How about you?

- If you're not sure of the other person's intent, can you give them the benefit of the doubt? Is there any reason why you can't or couldn't?

As you may recall, at the start of this chapter, I suggested that imagining what the other person's cost-benefit-future triangles could be behind something they said or did might be helpful to gaining an understanding of their perspective as well as insight into what may have motivated them to do whatever it was they did.

Questions for Re-thinking Violation

- What relationship rules or expectations did the other person break? If you broke one or more, which ones?
- Did the other person know that what they did was a violation? Is it possible that they didn't or couldn't have known? How about you?
- Have the two of you ever talked about the rules or expectations that were broken?
- How reasonable were these rules or expectations given the nature of your relationship?
- Are you both in agreement on what the nature of your relationship is?
- Are you both, then, mutually agreed on the rules of your relationship?
- As for the rule or rules that were broken, were you both in complete agreement on them; or did one or both of you assume it was something you were both totally agreed on?

- Where did the broken rule(s) come from? Are any rooted in one or more of your values?
- Do you share these values? (See Section 6.5.1 on values and resolving values conflicts.)
- How easy or hard would it be and what would it likely take for the both of you to change at least some of your rules or expectations, and abide by this change?

Questions for Re-thinking Responsibility

As I mentioned in Chapter 1, how much a person can or should be held responsible for their actions is often a matter of degree, with extenuating circumstances that can and should be considered. If you can't fault the other person outright for all your loss, or if both of you can share responsibility for it, then the potential for conflict is considerably reduced.

- Does the responsibility for your loss rest entirely with the other person?
- If not, how much responsibility do you think you—or maybe someone else as well—should take? For what part of your loss?
- Did the other person have a choice in doing what they did? Did you?
- Could you or the other person have known better?
- How could you or the other person have possibly known?
- Were or are there any extenuating circumstances for the other person? How about for the both of you?

Sometimes who's at fault becomes unimportant. This is a good sign if it genuinely does not matter to either of you.

> *Note too that you can use these LIVR re-thinking questions to look at past conflicts and perhaps see what happened in a different light.*

6.5 STEP THREE: DISAGREEMENT RESOLUTION

Conflicts are often resolved in Step Two, but sometimes points of disagreement can still stand in the way. As I mentioned in Chapter 2, conflict often involves one or more points of disagreement that either helped spark it in the first place or help keep it going.

The goal of Step 3 is to come up with solutions to any disagreements or sticking points that were not resolved in Step 2. Ideally, through this step both of you will be able to see each other's points of disagreement in a different light and perhaps also see some merit in each other's point of view. It is also possible that you end up having to live-and-let-live and agree to disagree. There are several things you're most likely to disagree on.

- Your disagreement can be around facts. For example: "Is it, or is it not true, that you broke a rule we agreed on?" or "It's now 9:30, didn't you say you were going to pick me up an hour ago!" People try resolving disagreements about facts by trying to either prove or disprove (or at least discredit) them. When facts can be proven or disproven, it is typically in favor of one person or the other; which is to say, one of you is right and the other is wrong. Not all disagreements about facts can be resolved by proving or disproving them, because sometimes it's just not possible to do that. Sometimes, neither of you can or will know the whole story.

- Related to disagreement around facts, there can also be disagreement over your recall of the facts; or more simply speaking, you both may have different versions of what happened. As I mentioned in Chapter 3, when you're in conflict it's hard to think outside the mood, and it's also hard to **remember** outside the mood. What this means is that selective memory on both of your parts is almost certain in every conflict.

- There's no simple solution to this, but when you hear the other person say something like: "That's not how I remember it!" don't automatically assume that this is some kind of evasive strategy. In fact, it could be as sincere a statement as any. Two people can have very different memories of the same event and be equally— and genuinely—sure of the accuracy of their recall. If both of you can acknowledge that neither's recollection of what happened is likely perfect, and if you can agree that the truth most likely lies somewhere in between, then that is enormously helpful.

- Disagreement can also come from lingering doubts or questions about the other person's side of the story (e.g, "Who said you could do that?" "Where did you say you went?" "That was a really long coffee you had with your ex! Are you sure you still don't have feelings for her?").

- Even when some facts are clear, disagreements can stem from differences in opinion about the facts. This includes differences in how significant certain facts are to you or the other person and what you think they mean. For example, "Sure, my ex and I spent a long time at the coffee shop. We were just catching up—it doesn't mean anything" or "OK, I admit it, I lied... but it was a white lie." These kinds of disagreements are often rooted in differences in values. I'll discuss resolving values conflicts in the next section.

- Although communication is our most powerful tool in conflict resolution, it's not perfect. As we all know, sometimes in the thick of a conflict words can fail us. So disagreement can sometimes arise over your choice of words as well as the meaning of those words.

Just as emotions can hijack our thinking, they can also hijack our vocabulary.

- Disagreement can also arise over differences in how you both perceive and describe the same thing. For example:
  - What you see as being self-confident the other person sees as arrogance.
  - What you see as flirtatious the other person sees as being friendly.
  - What you see as being stubborn the other person sees as being firm.
  - What you see as being kind the other person sees as being weak.
  - What you see as being open-minded the other person sees as being gullible.

Don't rely too much on adjectives. Always ground what you want to say about how someone acts in specifics (for example, double-check the specific flashpoints list in Chapter 3 for ideas). In other words, try to be specific and concrete in telling the other person what you would like them to stop doing, start doing and keep on doing, as well as what you're OK with and what you're not OK with.

As far as resolving disagreements goes, everything I said in the earlier section on communicating when in conflict applies. Here are some further suggestions to consider:

- *In conflict resolution, <u>the</u> absolute truth about what happened might not be reachable; however, there is always <u>a</u> truth that may be.* If both of you can agree on that truth, then it becomes the "close enough, or good enough" truth. This "good enough" truth is usually the middle ground—or compromise—between the two of you. The question sometimes arises whether it's worth it to both of you to try to find that "good enough" truth. It might also require a leap of faith for one or both of you in order to accept this truth, and if there's enough trust between you, you often can.

- Ask yourself just how important it is for you to be right with this person in this conversation. Sometimes, it is essential to be right, but sometimes it just feels good to be right, or at least to have the last word. If it's just a matter of wanting to be right because it feels good, think about what the potential cost to your relationship of wanting to be right might be. *Consider the **three quickie questions**:* What good could this do? What damage could this do? Is it worth it?

- One risk worth noting during this stage is that of finding more things to disagree on. Sometimes as you both try to find common ground and agreement on your points of disagreement, you end up finding more things to disagree on. Your disagreements pile up because you can't possibly resolve them all at once. As they pile up, what may have started out as a spat now feels like a train wreck. *So, try to handle only one disagreement at a time.*

- Some disagreements can only be resolved when one or both of you admit the truth, apologize, and offer to make amends for one another's loss. And in other cases, the solution to some disagreements may also come down to agreeing to disagree.

Agreeing to Compromise

A lot of the time the solution to your disagreement comes down to making some kind of deal or compromise. Compromise involves asking questions such as:

- What am I going to do differently from now on?
- What are you going to do differently?
- What are we going to do differently?
- What—if needed—will the new rules of our relationship be?

Adopting new rules and adjusting your expectations of one another and sticking to them means that you need to do things differently, and doing things differently takes effort. So, whatever changes you both agree on must be worth the effort for both of you. This almost always takes some negotiation, some give and take, and it may even require at least some rearranging of your relationship, which is covered in Section 6.5.2.

Disagreement does have an upside; namely, it is often only by trying to work through your disagreements that you get to know one another better, and breakthroughs in your relationship are made. *Furthermore, always keep in mind that whatever it is you disagree on, don't lose sight of what it is you do agree on.*

6.5.1 VALUES AND VALUES CONFLICTS

Some conflicts stem not so much from disagreement about the facts of the matter, but about differences in values. *Disagreements over values often show up as differences in attitudes, opinions, beliefs, and in the decisions people make and the actions they take.*

While differences in attitude, opinion and belief can certainly get heated, potentially more serious conflicts can arise when someone does something that goes against one of your values— or you do something that goes against one of theirs.

Your values reflect what you care about and what touches you. As with flashpoints and fireworks, values are primarily felt rather than thought, and like flashpoi.nts and fireworks, can range in how deeply they are felt. This means that your values can range from simply being preferences to being the principles that guide your life's major decisions and everything you stand for, and help form your "moral compass." *You can think of values—and the strength of your feelings about them—as what bonds your attitudes, opinions, and beliefs: The stronger the feeling, the stronger the bond.*

You can certainly think you're doing the right thing, but if it doesn't also feel right, it's not a value.

Your most deeply felt values are the ones that not only mean the most to you but also are the ones that, when striving to live by them, add meaning to your life. In fact, some of your values can be so deeply felt that they are, in effect, part of what makes you, you. Values are such an integral part of you that you rarely give them a lot of thought unless, for example, you're asked about them. To illustrate, consider taking a few minutes to do this exercise.

Putting Your Values into Words

For each of the following pairs of things choose the one you value more. For some pairs it will be an easy choice for you to make; for others it will be harder to decide between the two. When you can, go with your first instinct, or "gut" reaction and try not to overthink your choice. Be honest with yourself and remember, there are no right or wrong answers.

Very Important!

Choosing one does not mean you don't value the other at all—it's just that the one you choose you value more—even if it's by the narrowest of margins.

Which do you value more:

- ❑ Action or ideas?
- ❑ Optimism or realism?
- ❑ Putting yourself first or putting others first?
- ❑ Romance or practicality?
- ❑ Commitment or freedom?
- ❑ Feeling or thinking?
- ❑ Luxury or frugality?
- ❑ Work or play?
- ❑ Competition or cooperation?
- ❑ Trusting or making sure?
- ❑ Looks or functionality?
- ❑ Serenity or excitement?
- ❑ Justice or compassion?
- ❑ Art or science?
- ❑ Career or family?
- ❑ Time or money?
- ❑ What's fun or what's serious?
- ❑ Taking chances or playing it safe?
- ❑ Faith in God or faith in humankind?

I'm sure that for many of these pairs your choice came to you instantly and easily—they likely reflect your strongest values—the ones you have the greatest conviction in and care about the most deeply and passionately. For the others it wasn't as easy a choice. For several of these it's likely you had to pause and weigh your decision. There's also a good chance that you had to play out various "it depends" scenarios in your mind before one choice finally edged out the other.

> Interested in exploring your values and the values of your friends? Or, for that matter, the values of anyone you'd like to get to know a little better? Try the **Meet My Values** card game. It's a great way to learn a lot of meaningful things about one another and have a lot of fun doing it! Visit **www.theconflictresolvingnetwork.com** to find out more.

Reflecting on the choices you made, you can probably see that your values can have a lot of influence on your beliefs, opinions, and attitudes; as well as on, for example:

- What your fireworks are (e.g., what you find funny or inspiring) and what your flashpoints are (e.g., what angers or offends you).
- What things you're OK with and in your "comfort zone" and what things don't sit well with you (or that you'd never do).
- What you should or shouldn't do in one situation or another.
- What you hear in the news that gladdens, inspires, or delights you and what things disappoint, sadden, or infuriate you.
- What points of view and decisions that people make which you agree with, and those you don't.
- Who you like, admire, respect and trust, and who you feel the opposite toward.

How deeply you hold a value can also determine how influential it can be in forming the priorities and goals you set for yourself and the key decisions you make along the way to achieve those goals. For example, your values influence what you'll do for a living (e.g., art or science; action or ideas), what you'll look for in the things you buy and how you'll spend your money (e.g., luxury or frugality; looks or functionality) and what you'll do in your free time (e.g., serenity or excitement).

Values are shaped by many influences, including your culture, family, upbringing and friends, key events in your life, your age and stage in life as well as your temperament and personality. Some of your values may stay with you your entire life and some can change at different times and stages in your life. For example, in your twenties, you may value excitement over serenity, and in your seventies, serenity over excitement. If you're a parent and your kids are grown and have left home, you may come to value more "me time" (i.e., start valuing putting yourself first over others first).

Things can also happen in your life that can change your values. For example, you might value romance over practicality (or practicality over romance) until something happens that changes which one of these you value more. Also, you can hold a value but not always be able to live up to it as much as you'd like; for instance, you may value optimism over realism, but find that it often takes a lot of effort to be optimistic. In this case, optimism becomes something you choose to work on.

Although in many relationships you can be far apart in age, life experience, or where you come from, you can't be too far apart on values. This is because in any kind of relationship, your values will come into play and must match (or at least not clash) when making many of the dozens, hundreds—or even thousands—of decisions you will make together over time.

In a marriage for example, having closely matching values may not be all that important in deciding whether to make dinner at home or order in one night, but it is critical to being able to agree on such things as:

- what you spend your money on (and how much);
- how you spend your fun and quality time together; and,
- how you raise your children (or, for that matter, when— or even if—you have children).

The further apart you are on values, the harder it will be for you to agree on lots of things; and so, the harder it will be to get along. *Simply put, the closer you are in values, the more opinions, attitudes, beliefs, and decisions you will likely agree on and the more time you will spend in agreement and "being on the same wavelength." The further apart you are on values, the more things you'll disagree on, and the more time you're likely to spend arguing.*

General Points to Keep in Mind When You're in a Conflict Over Values

People don't always see things in the same way, and that's to be expected. We also don't all share the same values, and even when we do, we don't necessarily feel equally deeply about them. When we disagree with someone over values that we don't hold very deeply, we can often simply bounce viewpoints and ideas back and forth, maybe change one another's mind a little bit—or not—and, in either case, easily move on to another topic of conversation. Simply speaking, with values that are not that deeply felt—those that are closer to being preferences than principles—it's easier to accept differences and agree to disagree.

Disagreements over *deeply held* values are another matter;
and disagreements over deeply held values with strangers
are another matter still. These disagreements can become
conflicts that escalate quickly, sometimes in a matter of minutes.
One of the reasons for this is that when you don't know each
other well–or at all–it's unlikely that you have much in common,
or that you have much of a positivity account balance to draw upon,
and there won't be much of an incentive to reach an agreement.
At best, the conversation will be more of a debate than conversation,
and often not a particularly friendly one at that. If the debate
turns ugly and into a conflict, it'll likely go in circles, and leave you
both polarized (which means ending up further apart than
you were before), as well as feeling drained and frustrated.
Remember, civility is easily abandoned with strangers,
and even more so when you're both online and anonymous.

When you're close to the other person, and your relationship matters to you both, values differences can also be hard to resolve and can pose a challenge regardless of the type of relationship you're in. One of the reasons for this is that it can be especially disappointing when someone close to you differs on one or more values that you feel strongly about—in fact, it can feel like a betrayal or even an attack.

So let me begin with this: *No matter how hard it is for you to take what the other person said or did, try as best you can not to say anything right away. Instead, after a second or two, ask: "Do you want my opinion?" or "Do you want to know how I feel?" or "Do you want to know how I see things?"* This pause, and straightforward questions like these, gently invite the other person to pause too—and listen—and this can open the door to dialogue.

Along the same line, whether you've got a suggestion,
or some advice, or some constructive criticism you're thinking
of offering, it's generally a good idea to ask the other person if
they want to hear it first. Phrases like "May I make a suggestion?"
or "Can I give you some advice?" or "Want to know what I think?"
can work wonders.

Consider the following general points the next time you have a difference in values with someone (whether you know them well or not):

- Because values are things you feel, it's often hard to convince anyone to change their mind on a value they feel very strongly about (just as it's hard for anyone to change yours).

- Always remember, however, that no matter how deeply it is felt, you cannot "prove" a value. If you could, then, by definition, it'd be a fact and not a value. ***Values are not facts: The things that support your belief in a value can be facts, but that doesn't make the value a fact.***

- For instance, no one can prove that cooperation is better than competition, or that optimism is better than realism, or that romance is better than practicality. Each has their own plusses and minuses. So, try not to get drawn into a debate over whose value is better or "truer." This is an argument that is almost guaranteed to go nowhere but in circles.

- The most that you can say is that "it depends." For example, it may be that competition benefits some people more than others in some situations, and that cooperation benefits other people more in other situations. It might also be, for example, that optimism is more helpful than realism for some people in certain circumstances, and that realism is more helpful to other people in other circumstances.

- You can always back up your values, opinions, and beliefs with vivid accounts of what you yourself have experienced, other people's firsthand accounts, solid facts and statistcs, as well as sound reasoning. There is no doubt that all these things can prompt the other person to reconsider their point of view or at least see more merit in yours.

- However, always remember that even if your personal, as well as other people's stories are heartfelt and compelling, and even if your reasoning is sound, and your facts are rock solid, this does not mean that the other person will be persuaded to change their values (or attitudes or opinions or beliefs). Why? Because whatever it is you've experienced and whatever your facts and reasoning are, may not matter as much to them as they do to you.

- ***Bear in mind it's possible that whatever matters to you because of your values, may not matter as much to the other person because of theirs.***

- Taking competition versus cooperation as an example again: How much it matters to you who benefits more from competition than cooperation, why, and in what situations, might depend more on your values than on the facts themselves.

- Simply put, even if you can agree on all sorts of facts, you can end up disagreeing on what they mean and how much they matter. You might also disagree on what or who caused these facts to materialize, and by extension, who should take either the credit or the blame.

- Along the same line, someone may believe the facts you have, but given the values they hold, see these facts very differently. Facts do not always "speak for themselves;" and even when you think they do, what they say may be interpreted very differently by people whose values differ from yours.

- Note that when facts go against our values it's not unusual for us to question the credibility of the source of those facts. However, as with arguments about the rightness of one value over another, arguments over the credibility and trustworthiness of one source over another can also end up going in circles. This is true whether this source is a person (e.g., an expert, a well-known journalist, or a public figure) or an organization (e.g., a news channel or government department).

- Bear in mind, too, that once your mind is made up about a value, it's a lot easier to look for, pay attention to and remember things that back up your value as opposed to those things that contradict it. It's only natural to rarely, if ever, look for facts that contradict your values, attitudes, opinions, and beliefs, and ignore or downplay any that do. On this point, you and the other person are likely no different.

Just because you can see the biases or blind spots in someone else's point of view doesn't mean you don't have any yourself.

Finding Common Ground or at Least Partial Agreement

- When you disagree on a value, remember that it doesn't always mean that the other person doesn't value what you value at all, it's just that they don't value it as much as you do.
- Along the same line, it's important to say specifically whatever it is you do agree on, even if it's only partly. ***Some agreement is always better than no agreement.***

- Is it possible that you agree on the ends, but not the means? Let's say you agree on some universal ideal such as peace, justice, or equality, or a personal one, such as health, wealth, or the pursuit of happiness, but have different ideas about how any of these ideals can or should be achieved. Along the same line, you may agree on a problem or on what needs to be fixed, but not on how to fix it. In either case, it's easy to get the impression that your values are a lot further apart than they really are. ***Agreeing on a goal or an ideal, but not on how to achieve it, is a lot better than not agreeing on the goal in the first place.***

- Maybe you agree with what the other person says about a value at least to some extent, but not with ***how*** they're saying it. How someone says things can detract so much from ***what*** they're saying that it's hard to admit you agree with them even when you do. ***If that's the case, say so.*** As I mentioned earlier, when feelings run high, not everyone says what they mean or means what they say—and that includes how they say it.

- Similarly, perhaps you agree with some of what the other person is saying but feel that they're taking some things too far. If that's the case, say so.

- Although it's sometimes hard, showing respect for one another's values and points of view can work wonders. If you can't bring yourself to do that, then try, as best you can, not to show any disrespect. ***At the very least, if you can't respect the other person's value, then at least respect their right to have one.***

- Note too that the phrases: "With respect..." and "With all due respect, ..." can be especially helpful in any conversation.

- In a lot of conversations about values sooner or later the word "care" comes up. When someone says, "I care," this can certainly be a genuine and sincere statement about how they feel. But words like care, caring and so forth, can also be stretched in a lot of different directions and mean a lot of different things to different people. Remember:

- ○ We all care about some things, but not everyone cares about the same things.
- ○ Even when we care about some of the same things, we don't always care about them to the same degree.
- ○ There's a limit to the number of things any one of us can care about deeply. In other words, if you care about a lot of things, there's also a limit to how deeply you can care about any one of them.
- ○ When it comes to caring, you cannot spread yourself too thin without exhausting yourself emotionally sooner or later.
- ○ People can say they care about things that they either know nothing about or do nothing about (even if they could). One reason for this is that it's easy to say: "I care about _____." because people rarely ask for proof that you do. Moreover, because it sounds so good when you say, "I care," that when you say, "I don't care" you sound callous and hardhearted.

- So, bearing all this in mind, during any conversation about values:
  - ○ Avoid asking such loaded questions as: "Don't you care about _____?" "Why don't you care about _____?" or "How can you not care about _____?"
  - ○ If you're asked questions like these, remember you can care about something just as much as the other person but show it differently.
  - ○ You can also care just as much about something as the other person but disagree on what to do about it (e.g., if it's some problem or other you're talking

about). *Not agreeing about what to do about a problem does not necessarily mean not caring about it.*

- ○ Try your hardest to never utter such escalating and polarizing words as "I don't care!" "So what?" or "Who cares?" *It's usually not a matter of caring versus not caring; it's a question of how much.*

- Show as much empathy for how the other person feels as you can. Saying things like: "I understand what you mean", "I get where you're coming from" or "I get what you're saying" (if it's true that you do) can cool tempers, prevent escalation, and bring you at least a little bit closer.
- While empathy and understanding can go a long way to help resolve a values conflict, it is also important to remember that you can understand someone's point of view without necessarily agreeing with it.
- It's perfectly OK to tell the other person that you get how they feel and understand why they value what they value and why they believe what they believe—*but that you see things differently.*
- You may sometimes hear the other person say: "You're not listening!" If you are in fact listening, you may need to say something like: "I am listening to you, I'm just not agreeing." *Not agreeing is not the same thing as not listening.*

Key Things to Try to Avoid

- Try to avoid stating your values as though they are facts. One way to do this is to use I-statements (mentioned earlier in this chapter) such as: "The way I see it is...", "From my point of view...", "The way I feel about it is...", "For me the thing is...", or "In my opinion..."

- Resist using phrases such as: "It's just me..." or "It's only my opinion..." Using words like "just" or "only" in these cases can make it sound like you're inadvertently minimizing the importance of what you're saying because it's you who's saying it.

- When you believe that adhering to a value is the key to a better world, it's hard not to want others to share that value too, and so in a lot of situations, it's hard not to think of your value as being right and any opposing value as being wrong. This tendency is even built into ordinary language as when we say that something is the "right thing to do" or that we are making a "value judgement." Indeed, one of the most difficult things about having a conversation about values is the judgment of right and wrong that can fly in both directions. I know this is hard to do, but ask yourself: *In this case, can you and the other person both be right, but in different ways?*

- Try not to give the other person the impression that you think there's something wrong with them for not having the same value(s) as you. And whatever you do, try your hardest not to blurt out questions like: "What on earth is the matter with you?" or "What's wrong with you?"

- Along the same line, as best you can, try not to come across as morally superior or more virtuous because you value what it is you value more than the other person. Coming across as "holier-than-thou," for example, will almost certainly be a flashpoint for the other person.

- Don't assume that the other person doesn't understand what you're saying just because they disagree with what you're saying. Remember that in all likelihood, the other person is perfectly capable of both understanding and disagreeing at the same time. And if someone says to you: "You don't understand" you can always reply: "I understand what you're saying, I just don't agree with it."

- Avoid put-downs and name calling. Obviously, this applies to directly putting down and name calling the other person, but it also applies to those who the other person may admire. So, instead of saying, for example: "_____ is an idiot!" consider saying something like: "I think _____ has some good qualities, but I don't agree with _____."
- Be careful that you don't sound too pushy. If you sound too pushy it may seem to the other person that you're trying to cram your values and beliefs down their throat.

Additional Points to Consider if You Know Each Other Well

As mentioned earlier, it can certainly be very upsetting when someone close to you differs on one or more values that you feel strongly about; so, when that happens, in addition to considering the points made so far, consider asking yourself:

- Do the two of you absolutely have to agree on this value?
- How much does it really matter that the two of you differ on this value? Is this disagreement important enough to start what could potentially be a serious argument?
- If it's something the other person has done that goes against one of your values, how serious is that? Is it serious enough to say or do something or is live-and-let-live and agree to disagree the best thing to do?
- *To answer these questions, consider the three quickie questions:* What good could saying or doing something do? What damage could it do? Is it worth it?
- Are there plusses about the other person and your relationship that outweigh the fact that you differ as much as you do on this value? For example, do the two of you agree on more values than you disagree on, and if so, how much does that count?

- Do you like each other enough that both of you can overlook whatever values differences you have? In other words, can your liking for one another (i.e., your positivity account balance) offset any sense of loss this difference in values between you creates?
- Does the other person mean well? Do you both mean well? Even if you disagree, if you both mean well, doesn't that count for something?
- Is there something that matters to you, or the both of you, more than whatever the value is you're disagreeing on? That is to say, is there an overriding value, such as how much your relationship means to you, that outweighs how much it matters that you disagree?
- How far apart on this value are the two of you really? Value conflicts can be polarizing and when you're caught up in the heat of an argument, it can feel like you're further apart than you actually are.
- When you know the person well, calmly asking them *why* they value and believe what they do can be very helpful. There can sometimes be a very personal—and moving— story behind why they hold some of the values they do. That story may help you see and understand the other person and their thought processes in a whole new light.
- When someone feels understood in this way, they may not even need you to agree with them. ***A lot of people don't need agreement when they've got understanding and personal acceptance.***
- If you know the other person well enough to know at least some of their flashpoints, be mindful of them. With some people, there are some topics, such as politics, religion, sex, or money, that are just plain touchy, and should be steered clear of if you want to keep the peace. In fact, if you think about it, all of us have some touchy subjects that, when argued about with almost anybody,

are guaranteed to generate a lot more heat than light, no matter what.

Some Final Points to Keep in Mind When You're in a Conflict Over Values

In the end, how big a problem value differences with someone are depends on the values you differ on, how far apart you are, and how important they are to both of you. It also depends on the nature of your relationship and how important it is to you both that you agree on these values (and how distressing it is to you both that you don't). What also matters is the nature and importance of the decisions you must make together based on these values.

Of course, it's important to keep in mind that when the other person openly *agrees* with you on the values (and the related opinions and beliefs) you hold most deeply, this can be bonding and spark feelings of connection and mutual respect. Not only that, but if you're able to do things together that reflect some of those shared values, some real fireworks can come out of this! This is one of the reasons why, as I noted in Chapter 1, early on in any kind of relationship a good deal of time is spent figuring out how compatible you are on, among other things, your values.

Finally, it's also important to point out that differences in values don't always spell conflict. Some degree of difference between you and the other person on some values can be helpful and even fun (or at least make for some lively conversations). For example, if an idea or a decision based on the other person's values means doing something that's not too far out of your comfort zone, you could find yourself pleasantly expanding your horizons. Also, and again, if you're not too far apart, opposite values can attract or at least complement one another. For example, most idea-oriented people could use an action-oriented person by their side, and vice versa. Most optimists could occasionally benefit from the perspective of a realist, and vice versa.

6.5.2 RELATIONSHIP REARRANGING

As you may remember, in Chapter 2 I introduced the term structural conflict. As I said, most significant conflicts are of this type. Frequent arguments, fights, or all-out blow ups are signs of structural conflict. What makes structural conflicts different from transitory (or "one-off") conflicts is that there is usually a deeper, underlying conflict going on; that is to say, a conflict behind the conflict. This conflict behind the conflict likely comes from one or more aspects of the relationship being out of balance, meaning that something must change for its plusses to outweigh its minuses. In other words, with the way it is, the negatives of the relationship outweigh the plusses, which sets up the conflict.

Sometimes, a relationship cannot be what you'd planned or hoped it would be. It may have many plusses but not enough—or not enough of the ones you really want—to make it the kind of relationship you wish it were and think it could be. Although there are lots of strengths in the relationship, there's conflict because it does not completely meet what one or both of you want. When splitting up isn't something either of you want to do, one way to help prevent future conflicts is to rearrange your relationship.

The extent of rearranging required can vary a lot from situation to situation. In the simplest case, both of you agree to change one or two aspects of your relationship. This means basically coming to a compromise in which you both agree to try to do less of some things and more of other things. Simple relationship rearranging like this might mean adding or removing one or more items on your relationship menu (i.e., the topics you talk about, or things you do together or do for one another) or cutting back on the amount of time you spend together, texting or chatting less often, etc. Note that minor rearrangements like this often happen in all kinds of relationships without either of you even needing to talk about them.

Relationship rearranging can, however, involve more than making a few simple adjustments or compromises. Sometimes relationship rearranging involves making a lot of changes and can feel more like re-construction than rearrangement. Some examples of when significant relationship rearrangement is likely called for is when:

- a couple realizes that they cannot continue to be together as spouses, but want to remain partners in the raising of their children;
- you're in a conflict-prone relationship (e.g., a lop-sided, stretched or draining relationship) and want to get out of the pattern that you've both fallen into; or,
- a parent begins to realize that their child is no longer a child and therefore can no longer be treated like one.

In relationship rearranging, you try to keep what you can and want to keep, leaving behind whatever it is you don't want, and with what you've got left to work with, try to build a new kind of relationship. For relationship restructuring to work keep in mind that:

- Both of you must agree that rearranging your relationship is an option worth pursuing and you must also agree on what needs rearranging. Coming to this agreement can be difficult and even painful, as in the case of when couples are "decoupling." This can take a while, and because it often involves some trial-and-error, it means both of you are likely to make a few mistakes along the way.
- You must also agree on your new relationship's rules and expectations. This is a way of stopping or preventing conflicts from happening because by agreeing to new rules and expectations you're basically redefining what it means for there to be a loss or a violation. Specifically, you need to agree on:
  - What's on—and what's not on—your relationship menu—and especially, what fireworks are no longer on your relationship menu.

- How you are both supposed to act toward one another, and what flashpoints you both must try to avoid setting off in one another.
- What new things both of you are expected to do for one another.
- What things you are no longer expected to do for one another.
- What both of you can continue to expect from one another.

- Rearranging may also have to take into consideration others—especially those who matter to you the most— and any impact it may have on them. If this is the case, the rearranging itself may have to also include rearranging the relationship between, for example, the other person and those closest to you.
- Relationship rearranging often means more than just changing relationship rules; it can mean changing your roles as well, and along with your roles, the "scripts" or patterns that go with those roles. Again, this can take a while and involve some trial and error.
- Changing scripts means changing not only what you talk about, but—and often more importantly—*how* you talk to one another. Changing long-standing patterns may also be necessary.
- Changing a long-standing pattern of relating to one another is not easy, nor is coming up with new rules and adjusting your expectations of one another and sticking to them. It will take effort. Whatever changes you agree on must be worth the effort for both of you, which will invariably take some negotiation, compromise and making trade-offs that must work for both of you.
- When making trade-offs, if you both like and dislike the same things, then compromise can be relatively easy.

Where relationship rearranging gets more complicated is when each of you must give up some things you like and accept some things you don't like. So, carefully consider the following:

- What do you want from this relationship that you haven't got or haven't got as much of as you'd like?
- What needs to change for this relationship to work for you?
- Do you deserve better? Can you do better?

What you want in a relationship often depends on what you think you can get.

- What can you <u>give</u> in return?
- What can you <u>give up</u> in return?
- What is it that you can give or give up that wouldn't cost you a lot ***but*** would mean a lot to the other person? *In other words, are there any things that wouldn't cost you that much to give (or to give up) but would mean the world to the other person?*

- Note that for either of you to be OK with whatever it is you give or give up, what's left has to be enough to keep the plusses ahead of the minuses. If this is the case and it works for both of you, then relationship rearranging can pave the way to successfully moving forward in almost any relationship. Make sure you both are agreed on how to move forward, which means being clear on what both of you are ready to commit to, and, as I mentioned earlier, both agreeing to what's on—and what's not on—your new relationship menu. It is essential that both of you are not only 100% agreed on your agreement, but that you are also 100% clear and agreed on exactly what it is you've agreed to.

- Finally, if it makes sense, consider whether the rearrangement you've agreed to is to be permanent or not. Maybe a trial period would work. In any case, relationship rearrangement doesn't always have to be permanent. In some cases, there may be things that you just don't want to do with one another anymore right now but might be willing to reconsider at some point in the future.

6.6 STEP FOUR: RECONCILIATION AND CELEBRATION

It feels great when you resolve your conflict; and, as I noted in Chapter 2, this last step of the conflict resolution process can be transformative for your relationship and is often "sealed" or celebrated with a handshake, a hug, going for a drink or kissing and making up (depending on the relationship). It can also be "trajectory-changing" and can be a marvelous new beginning and a fresh start.

Moments of reconciliation and celebration after a conflict can add a lot to your positivity account with the other person. In beautiful moments like this a lot of bad feelings can be completely dissolved.

Another hallmark of this last step of the conflict resolution process is closure, which is typically felt by both of you. Closure means not only putting a resolved conflict to rest, but also successfully resolving your questions and feelings around it.

Closure can be arrived at in many ways; and each of the four steps of the conflict resolution process can contribute to it. For example, closure can be reached by finally hearing the truth, or admitting the truth; by apologizing and making amends for past wrongs, receiving an apology owed to you; or more generally, by finally saying or doing something that you have wanted to say or do for a long time—something that finally expresses your bottled-up thoughts and feelings, or that removes the uncertainty (or even ambivalence) that typically hangs over issues that you want closure on.

Closure can be immediate and complete (like an on/off switch), but more often than not it takes time and is a gradual process. The following are some telltale signs that either your conflict is not fully resolved or that you have not yet reached full closure on everything that happened:

- You feel more relief than joy and there's little or no joy in your celebration. ***Relief is not the same thing as joy.***
- You have a lingering sense of mistrust or worry and get the feeling that you may have rushed into agreeing or saying: "It's ok.", "It's all good.", "I forgive you.", or something along these lines, a little too soon.
- You're still replaying the conflict in your mind; and often with tinges of regret. For example, you start second-guessing yourself and ruminating about what you or the other person could have done differently, should have done differently, or would have done differently if.... And as you mentally replay these scenarios you sometimes start triggering inner escalation, which can get you very wound up.
- Memories of problems in the relationship, such as the flashpoints you'd forgotten about, start popping up.
- Particularly if it was a serious conflict, it's not unusual for one or both of you to have lingering doubts. This can last for a while, or until enough trust in one another returns. For at least a while, then, both of you may be on "high alert" for signs of real change in the way you treat one another.

Sometimes you can't fully resolve a conflict on your first attempt. However, if you've made some progress, it is certainly a step in the right direction. It's important to remember too that even when a conflict isn't or can't be fully resolved, there's a good chance that you've managed to lessen its impact for all concerned.

6.6.1 ON FORGIVING AND ASKING FOR FORGIVENESS

> *"To err is human, to forgive divine"*
> ALEXANDER POPE
> (ENGLISH WRITER, 1688-1744)

As with apology, asking for forgiveness and forgiving are integral to conflict resolution. Indeed, it is hard to think of anything sweeter and anything more beautiful in conflict resolution than forgiveness. There's power in forgiveness for you and for the person who has wronged you. It frees you of the emotional burden of flashpoint feelings such as anger, resentment or hurt, and brings with it a sense of peace and often joy. Forgiveness also brings closure to the conflict and allows you—and in many cases the other person—to move on. What follows are points to consider whether you're the one being asked to forgive or the one asking for forgiveness.

If You're the One Being Asked to Forgive

- All emotions fade over time; and, like any emotion, your sense of loss diminishes over time. Although time can and does reduce psychological loss, in some cases it may never completely erase it. This is one of the things that can make forgiveness difficult. When enough time has passed, many things are easier to forgive and as more time passes, easier and easier to forgive.

- Accepting someone's apology typically comes with forgiving them. But it doesn't have to.

- You can still have some kind of relationship with someone, even if you haven't fully forgiven them for what they did.

- ***Forgiveness rarely means forgetting what happened, but it often means forgetting the bad feelings around what happened.*** Forgetting in the case of forgiving is not necessarily amnesia for what happened.

- If you forgive the other person, say it out loud—"I forgive you for _____."

- Similarly, as I said earlier in this chapter, never say: "All is forgiven." when all is not forgiven.

- It is also possible to forgive someone without them knowing (or ever knowing), or when you know an apology is never forthcoming or when the person has passed on.

- Sometimes you want to forgive, but you just can't. Or at least you can't yet. Give yourself time. If you're not ready yet to forgive, remember that you can't push yourself to forgive the other person. For that matter, you can't push the other person to forgive you either.

On Understanding and Forgiveness

There is no doubt that understanding is very helpful in conflict resolution. For example, coming to a better understanding of one another's point of view can be helpful, as can understanding why someone treated you badly. Understanding can increase your empathy and even sympathy for the other person and may help you see their intent and what was behind what they did a little differently and perhaps with a little less anger and a little more compassion. So, because of these things, understanding can make forgiveness easier.

All these are good things; however, as I said earlier, never let your understanding be interpreted as excusing, justifying, or permitting the other person's treatment of you. Furthermore, just because you understand why the other person does something that, for example, hurts you time and time again, doesn't mean you have to accept or put up with it. ***Understanding does not necessarily mean agreeing with what the other person says or does, nor does it mean putting up with how they treat you.***

Understanding and forgiveness are two different things. Understanding may help you forgive someone, but it does not obligate you to forgive. Forgive when and if you are ready. ***Always remember that there is a limit to how understanding and empathic you can—or for that matter—should be.***

You can develop understanding toward someone, and empathy as well as sympathy for them and their situation. However, there can come a point at which it no longer matters how much understanding you have and how much you feel for someone. Sometimes there are just too many minuses (e.g., flashpoints) and not enough plusses (e.g., fireworks) to sustain a relationship.

Forgiveness does not mean that the relationship continues as it was, or that it continues at all.

If You're the One Asking for Forgiveness

- Part of apologizing is often asking for forgiveness; so, make sure that before asking for forgiveness, you apologize first. Just as it's critical to be clear what you're apologizing for, be clear in your mind about what it is you are asking forgiveness for and say it out loud.

- Forgiveness can be total and almost immediate, as when you let bygones be bygones. But it isn't always total or immediate; sometimes fully forgiving someone is gradual and can take a long time, even years.
- Although it can be hard to accept, it is possible that you won't be forgiven, or at least not right away.
- When or if you are forgiven, remember that it may take the other person a long time to fully trust you again. You will need to re-earn their trust.
- Remember that some people are more forgiving than others and that there are some things that some people may never forgive.

6.7 FAMILY, FRIENDS, AND OTHERS IN CONFLICT RESOLUTION

Just as there are some problems in life that are hard to solve without someone's help, there are some conflicts that could benefit from a helping hand. This is where family, friends, and sometimes, professionals come in.

When you're in conflict with someone, it's only natural to turn to those you trust such as friends or family. Sometimes those you turn to know the person you're in conflict with and sometimes they don't. When they don't know the other person, or don't know them very well, then it's likely that they'll be hearing only your side of the story. If this is the case, then one potential downside to seeking support or advice from friends and family is that they'll likely automatically side with you. This isn't necessarily a bad thing, and despite not being able to see both sides of the story, friends and family members might see things in a different way than you and have some good advice to offer.

*"The go-between wears out a
thousand sandals."*

JAPANESE PROVERB

When those you turn to know both of you, they might be able to
see things about you as well as the other person that neither of you
can. They can also be helpful as go-betweens. As I mentioned earlier, when you're considering offering an olive branch, mutual
friends might be able to smooth any ruffled feathers in advance of
your offer. Even if they can't give much in the way of advice, or
help in any other concrete way, sometimes they can be a sympa-
thetic sounding board and just listen.

So, how can professionals help? Given their neutrality compared to your friends and family, as well as their experience in
helping people resolve their conflicts, professionals such as
counselors, couples' counselors and mediators can help in a lot of
ways. How they can help specifically depends on their areas of expertise, the nature of the conflict you're in, and whether you're
approaching them alone or together with the person you're in conflict with. In addition to whatever they can help with specifically,
professionals can often help lessen the impact of your conflict on
you, on the other person and those who matter to you the most.

CONCLUDING THOUGHTS

As I wrote in the preface of this book, conflict is an inevitable part of our lives and perfectly natural in the ebb and flow of any relationship. But, with every successful resolution of a conflict, you change where and how far your relationship might go—regardless of the kind of relationship it is. In other words, you change both its outlook and its potential. Even a small change in the way you relate to one another now can lead to progressively more significant and lasting change in your relationship as time goes on. *In fact, even the tiniest difference can make all the difference.* Immediately, though, you should see some effects of successfully having resolve a conflict. For example:

- There's a new understanding that's emerged between you and a new capability to understand one another;
- You're learning to disagree with one another without being disagreeable;
- There's greater trust and respect, and better communication between you (e.g., you're better able to give each other the chance to say what either of you feels needs to be said);
- You appreciate one another more (e.g., you appreciate it when you see each other making the effort to do better);

Sometimes seeing the other person make a genuine effort is enough.

- You feel more confident in your relationship generally, and that you'll both be able to handle future conflicts better; and,
- If you still need to fix or rearrange some aspect of your relationship, you're both confident that you can do it.

Simply put, you're further ahead in your relationship now than you were before.

Not only are these great indicators of how far you've come, but there are also some other sure signs of progress to look for in the weeks, months, and even years ahead:

- You have fewer and fewer conflicts as time goes on; and when they do happen, they're over sooner, less intense, and less damaging.
- More and more often, you catch yourselves before falling into old conflict-prone patterns and stop before the conflict gets very far (e.g., you catch—and stop— yourselves from escalating).
- After resolving a conflict when you do have one, your relationship not only bounces back faster, but rebounds to a higher level of trust and connection than ever before. Also, note that the time it takes for your relationship to rebound or for the both of you to recover emotionally from a conflict is an excellent indicator of its resilience.
- You don't have conflicts about the same things over and over again.
- You're both less hard on yourselves and each other when you have a conflict.
- You both learn more and more from the conflicts you have, as well as about one another.

- You get better and better at resolving your conflicts, which also carries over to being better at resolving conflicts with others.
- You have fewer flashpoint moments and more frequent fireworks moments with one another, which more than make up for whatever flashpoint moments you have.
- All in all, you're both happier and your relationship is better in the ways that matter the most.
- All things considered, you both feel that whatever it took, and however long it took, was worth it to get to where you are now.

Yes, there will continue to be ups and downs, and that's perfectly normal. Always remember, that the quality of any relationship depends not on the absence of conflict, but on how well the two of you can resolve it when it does arise. Learning to resolve your conflicts with someone who matters to you can take a while. I encourage you to be as patient as you can be, and to remember that even the longest journey doesn't seem so long if you can make occasional stops along the way and see how far you've both come.

Acknowledgments

I'd like to thank my colleagues who so generously gave of their time and expertise reviewing this book. They have contributed in many ways, and from a wide range of professional perspectives, including psychology, education, and human resource management, as well as leadership and executive coaching. Collectively, they represent decades of trusted experience in helping children, teens, adults, couples, families, and workplaces resolve countless conflicts. I am profoundly grateful for their insights and suggestions that have contributed so much to this book.

In particular, I'd like to thank: Kosala Abeygunawardena, Ade Adesina, Chris Aristides, Kimia Ashori, Mohammed Askari, Mona Atrzadeh, Kenny Baldwin, Susan Barrette, Jessie Bhatia, Charity Barfoot, Isabella Bergagnini, Anna Bonato, Nadia Bulbulia, Alessia Caputo, Rana Cassar, Victoria Creighton, Jo-Ann DeLuca, Paola Denegri, Jennifer Denny, Žana Dragovich, Aarti Gupta, Anthony Fallico, Oksana Halkowicz, Sarah Hallett, Gwyneth Humphreys, Sanam Karimizad, Anna Kriewald, Joyce Lai, Sandra Leckie, Gary Lilwah, Tara McAlpine, Anahita Meraj, Bahar Mobebbi, Laura Moore, Shiva Mortazavi, Victoria Moskovskaya, Nathan Pillai, Kristen Piggot, Samuel Rousseau, Samira Sadat Forghani, Sarvin Sabet Ghadam, Ahmad Sakkijha, Sohel Shivji, Maria Slutski, Kara Steyaert, Tia Sternat, Melissa Tawadros, Michael Tighe, Ivan Tran, Saida Valiyeva and Roja Vivekanand.

I would also like to thank my fellow faculty members and students at the Adler Graduate Professional School in Toronto, where I've had the honor and privilege of serving as a professor of psychology since 2014. The AGPS community has truly been a constant source of inspiration to me. Finally, I'd like to thank my friends for their unfailing encouragement: A.E., B.I., C.M., I.R., K.L.M., L.A., M.P., P.B., S.S., S.W. and T.R.L.

I Welcome Your Feedback

For me, writing this book was a four-and-a-half-year labor of love. In the end, though, it isn't about me: It's about how helpful my book has been to you. So, naturally, I'd love to hear how my book has helped you and those who matter the most to you resolve your conflict. But just as importantly, because I am committed to making The Four Essentials of Conflict Resolution better with every edition, I'd also like to hear what you think I could have covered that I didn't, or what topics I could have covered in more detail, or what points are not clear, or which you think could be expanded upon.

Please send me any comments, thoughts,
or suggestions you have by visiting
www.theconflictresolvingnetwork.com

Whatever you say will be kept completely confidential, and your email address will never be sold or shared. Although I can't reply to everyone who writes in, please be assured every comment or suggestion you make will be read.

About the Author

Dr. Lodzinski holds a Ph.D. in applied social psychology from the University of Windsor and is a professor of psychology at the Adler Graduate Professional School in Toronto, Ontario. He has contributed to many fields in his career including the arts, education, health and wellness, as well as career development. Additionally, over the last 15 years he has focused on conflict resolution working with individuals, couples, families as well as workplaces, and has trained well over 200 professionals in his approach to conflict resolution. He makes his home with his family in Toronto.

www.ingramcontent.com/pod-product-compliance
Lightning Source LLC
Chambersburg PA
CBHW021356090426
42742CB00009B/879